The Prisoner

An Invitation to Hope

Paul F. Everett

Paulist Press
New York/Mahwah, N.J.

Cover design by Stefan Killen
Book design by Lynn Else

Library of Congress Cataloging-in-Publication Data

Everett, Paul (Paul F.)
    The prisoner : an invitation to hope / Paul F. Everett.
        p. cm.
    Includes bibliographical references.
    ISBN 0-8091-4301-1 (alk. paper)
    1. Townsend, Jim, 1927- 2. Prisoners—United States—Biography. 3. Capuchins—United States—Biography. I. Title.
    BX4705.T7353E84 2005
    271'.3602—dc22

                                                2004020937

Published by Paulist Press
997 Macarthur Boulevard
Mahwah, New Jersey 07430

www.paulistpress.com

Printed and bound in the
United States of America

Preface

I realized that I was studying Brother Jim, who was sitting across from me at the luncheon table in the refectory of the Capuchin Hermitage, a contemplative friary of the Capuchin Franciscan Province of Saint Augustine. Saint Francis, the founder of the Franciscan Order, spent much of his time in caves and hermitages. This hermitage in which I was now sharing a meal was established to reclaim that contemplative vision of Saint Francis.

Jim, as usual, had finished eating before everyone else and his arms, in the big sleeves of his brown habit, were predictably folded across his chest. He then held court, sharing one humorous experience after another, while the other brothers and priests and I continued to eat.

I had met Jim a year and a half earlier (in 1991) when I first came to the Hermitage for reflection, prayer, and spiritual direction, which I did for two days every six weeks or so. During this much-needed personal time and space from a very demanding ministry and lifestyle, I would have, in addition to mealtimes with Jim, some brief periods of conversation with him.

In that first year and a half of knowing Jim, I took bits of information overheard at meals, as well as some remarks made to me from time to time in conversation, and pieced together an awareness that Jim had spent time in prison. I also concluded that everyone at the Hermitage and in the surrounding community knew Jim's story except me. Since it really was none of my business, I felt that I shouldn't pursue the subject. Yet, if my conclusions were actually true—that he had in fact been in prison—I knew there must be a tremendous story there. What had happened? What *was* the story? These questions increasingly and relentlessly intrigued me.

One afternoon when I was meeting for spiritual direction with Father Lester Knoll, the superior (or in Capuchin Franciscan terms, guardian) of the Hermitage, I finally brought up the subject. I had heard that Jim had just returned from speaking at Rockview State Correctional Institute at Bellefonte, Pennsylvania, and that he was a speaker much sought-after in prisons in Pennsylvania and beyond. I asked whether it was true that Brother Jim had spent time in prison. Father Lester told me that my conclusions were correct. He told me that when Jim was twenty years old he had murdered his wife, who was six months pregnant with twins.

Through the months that followed this disclosure, as I would come to the Hermitage for retreat, a trust level developed between Jim and me, and I slowly began to hear more and more of the story from Jim's own lips. The more I heard, the more overwhelmed I was by the story and the more difficult it was to grasp it all. I was unable to understand the depth of the dysfunctional conditioning of his early life that would lead him to kill someone he loved. I was fighting the disbelief that there could be anything good or positive left in Jim upon which a new life could be created. Yet, there was no denying that Jim was a changed man, a change that had long since been documented through his influence in the community and his work in prisons.

In the months afterward, I was not only hearing from others that Jim's experience should be told, but I, too, was growing in the same conviction. Inmates, their families, and people employed in prison work might find renewed hope through his story. (According to "America's Prison

Generation," a feature in *Newsweek*, November 13, 2000, 14 million Americans are in U.S. prisons.) Then, of course, there are millions of people imprisoned in countless other ways whose lives need to be changed and redirected.

However, I was unprepared one afternoon in 1996 when Father Lester asked me to consider writing the account of Jim's pilgrimage. He stated that he had liked the articles I had written in journals and other publications. He believed that I needed to expand my writing experience and, because I had known Jim for the past six years, he felt that I should and could write his story. He said, "This will be a great opportunity for you and it may help others to find help and direction for their lives. But," he added, "I can't pay you a cent. Will you do it?"

There was no question in my mind that this story had to be told, but I had never written anything like it before. I had no confidence that I could take the enormity of Jim's story and present it in a way that people would understand and in it find meaning for their own lives. After several weeks of struggling over the decision, I accepted the challenge. I realized that I had been so blessed by Jim through the years that I wanted to be part of telling one of the most powerful stories I had ever heard about what God could do with a human life.

As I continued to talk with Jim, I was overwhelmed with the awareness that somehow I was on holy ground. In knowing more about him and the impact of his life on the contemplative community in which he was living, I believed that I was going to be challenged spiritually at a depth I had never known. My conviction was right on target.

Through the life of Jim Townsend, I was made aware in a deeper way that God's love for us is unchanging and is never altered by anything we have ever done. No act of ours is beyond his forgiveness and no life is beyond his ability to change and redirect.

Jim once said to me, "Paul, I thought my life was over when I went to prison. I wanted it to be over. I had a self-hate that was all consuming. All I can say is that if God could get to me, he can get to anybody. He gave me a hope and a future. What more is there than that!"

A friend of mine once said that God can take an ordinary life and do extraordinary things with it. Jim Townsend is such a person whose life, once redirected by God, has been used in extraordinary ways. This is his story.

Paul Everett
March 2004
"Woodland"
Sherman, Connecticut

Acknowledgments

One of the greatest gifts I was finally willing to accept is the ability to receive from others. From my earliest remembrance I was conditioned to believe that to rely on or receive help from another was an indication of weakness and inadequacy. I thank God for the moment when I realized I could be part of the human race and enjoy the fullness of relationships—the ability to receive as well as give.

This moment of realization has been with me constantly since I was challenged to write *The Prisoner* because I know that I couldn't have done it without the help and encouragement of some very significant people in my life. Some of these people I had known for some time, others I had yet to meet, but both would become essential in my meeting this challenge.

My wife, Maggie, my first editor, who agonized for years over the scholastic papers and articles I had written, enthusiastically encouraged me to write *The Prisoner*. She has not only typed but also scrutinized every word in this book, from first to last. She has kept me focused and has encouraged me at every turn.

Father Lester Knoll, Capuchin Franciscan, my spiritual director and mentor, is the person who initially challenged me to write this book. He constantly reassured me when I became discouraged and challenged me to keep at it. He believed in me and my ability to tell Jim's story. It is to him that I dedicate this book.

Connie Miner, my secretary during my time as Executive Director of the Pittsburgh Experiment, initially transcribed all the tape interviews, which were essential in establishing the chronology of the events of Jim's life. Connie's son, Mark, who had always encouraged me to write and who, with his own writing skills, supervised my contribution to a project for the *Pittsburgh Business Times,* was another loud voice from my cheering section—"You can do it."

Ptolemy Tompkins, Senior Editor of *Guideposts,* used his proven editorial skills and his "red ink" margin notes to help inform the format of this book. His patience with me, his affirmation of Jim's story, and his "Go after it, Paul," kept me keeping on.

Also of *Guideposts* is Elizabeth Gold, Managing Editor of Books and Inspirational Media, who was among the first to read the finished manuscript. She gave me hope with her enthusiastic response but also intrigued Janet Kobobel Grant to become my agent. Janet's patience, perseverance, and teaching have been essential for now and for the future.

Guideposts friends Rick Hamlin, Executive Editor; Edward Grinnan, Editor-in-Chief, and John Temple, CEO, provided essential advice regarding the writing of such a story.

Arthur Caliandro, author and minister of Marble Collegiate Church in New York City, pursued his contacts on my behalf and critiqued the manuscript. Paula D'Arcy, author and longtime friend, challenged me during times of discouragement to think of Jim's life and the power that transformed him. She gave me the benefit of her considerable writing skills and sensitivity as she read the manuscript.

My brother-in-law, John M. Allen, former Senior Editor and Vice President for Corporate and Public Affairs at the Reader's Digest, not only helped critique the format, but also made me aware of the enormity and difficulty of the project. Nevertheless, he encouraged my resolve that I had to do the best that I could do.

Pat Mulligan, a member of the Secular Franciscans, began a ministry to prisoners in 1992 and since that time has orchestrated mission teams going into prisons to conduct weekend retreats and special conferences. Jim Townsend has been an essential part of this special ministry. Pat's endless resource of stories of Jim's impact on prisoners is crucial for this book. I wish that we could have used all the stories provided, but I trust that those that were chosen convey the thoughts in the hearts of all the people whose lives Jim has touched. How grateful we are for Pat's ministry to Jim, for her management of his outreach to prisoners, and for the contribution of her firsthand knowledge of Jim, which greatly edifies these pages.

And finally I want to thank Brother Jim Townsend himself for his openness and honesty with me as he shared his story. His life and ministry have brought hope and healing to thousands of people, including myself.

PROLOGUE

The Arraignment

Gray and heavy was the cloud cover. It was a cold and sunless winter day, typical of southwestern Pennsylvania, where the sun rarely shines from mid-October until April. The grayness of the day seemed to envelop and make almost invisible the most imposing buildings in the Uniontown skyline. The Fayette County courthouse, a monolithic, turreted, Victorian structure, made of large-block graystone, and the adjoining jail, both with their weathered and stained facades, lost their dominance.

Inside the jail, the dinginess of the paint replicated the darkness of the day outside. In one of the jail cells in that structure sat a young man whose heart and spirit were being smothered by heaviness he had never before known. It was January 30, 1948, and James Townsend was about to face charges of first-degree murder in the killing of his wife, who was six months pregnant. The murder had occurred on November 13, 1947, at 9:30 p.m. in an old farmhouse in Bidwell Hollow near Ohiopyle, Pennsylvania.

Jim sat on his bunk in the dead silence of his jail cell, exhausted and numb, waiting to be escorted to the adjoining courthouse. This was the day of his arraignment. What would be the verdict? Had all of this really happened? He stared at the floor, head in his hands, totally numb. He thought, *I must be dead. I'm numb enough to be dead. Why don't I feel nothin'? I really don't care about nobody or nothin' any more.* He saw himself standing on the sidelines, watching a big hurricane churning inside himself, bombarded by clashing thoughts and feelings that he couldn't

3

touch. Armies of terrifying pictures of the murder, and flash-backs to a whole life of being scared, marched in his head. The silence of his cell, however, came to an abrupt end, and his awakened pulse brought feeling back into his lifeless self as he heard the guards enter the cell block, finally stopping and unlocking his cell door. The clanging noise reverberated off the institutional gray walls. There was nothing soft to absorb the sharpness of that sound.

Jim shuffled out of his cell, and the sheriff and his two deputies led him to the courthouse. He was surprised that he wasn't in handcuffs and chains. As he looked down at his clothes, he remembered a story about a man on the way to his trial demanding a suit, shirt, and tie "to look proper." He went into the courtroom and won. Jim, on the other hand, was dressed in a pair of overalls and a blue denim shirt. The clothes felt as if they had never been washed. They smelled institutional, but they were all he had.

These thoughts were quickly interrupted as he realized that he and his guards had finally reached the much heard-about "Bridge of Sighs," a long hallway that connected the jail to the courthouse, about ten-feet high, twelve-feet wide, and thirty- to forty-feet long, with a few small windows on each side. The "Bridge of Sighs" seemed to be an endless walkway to all prisoners who traveled it, for in the court-room behind the doors at the other end, they would learn their fate. Jim took a deep breath and started across the "bridge." When he finally walked into the courtroom, he was surprised at its appearance. Its wood-paneled walls and numerous windows gave it the feeling and warmth of a liv-ing room. It was such a contrast to the coldness he felt all around him. In the front of the room there was a high bench where the judge sat, with a jury box to the right. In front of the judge's bench were two tables, one for the prosecution and one for the defense. Then there was a railing with seats behind it. He further observed that there were three judges sitting at the bench. He reflected, *The presiding judge, he's a handsome guy. I wonder how old he is. The other guys look as neutral as it gets. In my dirty overalls in this place, I really do feel like nothin'.*

The arraignment began. The county had appointed two lawyers for Jim. They read all the material given to them, which concerned not only the murder but also Jim's history, a lifelong record of reform schools and jails for all kinds of assault offenses, one of which included attempted rape. The lawyers had told Jim that he should plead guilty. But here, in the courtroom, when the judge asked, "How do you plead?" he defiantly said, "Not Guilty." The lawyers made it clear that if he pled "Not guilty" and submitted to a jury trial, he could be sentenced to death. The district attorney, in an attempt to regain control, stated, "You are trying to get people to think you are insane. Remember, we had you tested by the psychologist and there is no doubt that you are perfectly sane."

Jim folded his arms across his chest, closed his eyes, and refused to answer any questions. The judge said, "You have to answer the questions." With those penetrating eyes that dominated his newspaper pictures, Jim looked at the judge and stated defiantly, "I won't answer the questions until you can prove that *you* are sane! I want to know about you first."

The judge made it clear that a contempt of court would follow any further refusal to answer the questions. At that moment Jim caught the sheriff looking at him and grinning, seeming to enjoy watching him have to submit to the authority of the court. The sheriff's mannerisms, interpreted by Jim as condescending, brought up painful memories of how his younger brother Bob would get him into trouble with their father or some other authority, and then enjoy watching him squirm.

The arraignment moved quickly and inevitably to every detail of the murder. He was forced to look at pictures of what he had done to Alice, his wife. He had to look at her naked body lying on the floor in the blood pouring from her fatal wound. He had to look at her opened, terrified eyes staring up at him from the picture—the very image that so haunted him the night of the murder when he literally shot her out of the tub onto the floor.

The *Pittsburgh Post Gazette,* on Friday, January 30, 1948, in describing the arraignment, reported that when the district attorney, Arthur Brown, showed Jim the picture of his wife's body, he knocked it out of his hand and started to get up. He had planned to make a break for it, or to commit suicide. Jim was quoted in the article, "Had it not been for Sheriff Echard moving close to me and other officers on guard nearby, I would have jumped out the third-story window. I might have killed myself or I might have escaped—either would have been satisfactory to me." But that did not happen. Information concerning Jim's plan had come to Warden Jack Cochran from other prisoners to whom he had confided. When the judge declared a ten-minute recess so that Jim could gain some self-control, the guards took him to the men's room and gave him a cigarette. They never left his side.

Back in the courtroom the arraignment continued. The prosecutor made him go through the whole incident again—more pictures, more details. In Jim's comments to the prosecutor he said, "It's kinda' hard to explain about the killing, you know. I was a bit drunk when all this happened with my wife. I'm not trying to get out of anything 'cause I definitely am guilty of killing my wife, you know, but as far as I'm concerned I'm not guilty of first-degree murder. But with my criminal record and my stupidity and meanness and all of that, they just put it down that way. But I can still remember when I shot my wife, and she was lyin' there bleeding—it sobered me up like you wouldn't believe. I was paralyzed. I don't care who you are, when you see a sight like that, you never forget it. What I couldn't get away from were her eyes. They stared at me. Those eyes were always there, and the blood, the blood, the blood. I was so jammed up inside with so many terrifying thoughts and feelings. Did I do this really? How could it have happened?"

The original story Jim told to the police was that he was upset with Alice and wanted to get away from things at the house so he thumbed a ride into Uniontown. Finding a saloon, he went in and entered a poker game that was already going on. After a hand or two, he felt that he was being set up by one of the men. With his typical aggressive attitude, he stood up to confront the men, but that's as far as it got. All three of the men picked him up and threw him out the window. Angry and bitter, he walked the ten miles back to the farm. Without a word he stormed into the house, grabbed his rifle, and started back out the door. Alice, realizing that he was up to something, tried to stop him. Jim pushed her away—the rifle went off—and she fell to the floor.

The *Uniontown Morning Herald* told what finally became the real story. On Saturday, November 15, 1947, a banner front-page headline stated, "Youth Admits Slaying of Wife Nearby." Under the headline was a large photograph of the isolated farmhouse in which the murder had taken place. Inserted in the lower left of the picture was a headshot of James Townsend, showing his rugged, good-looking face.

The lead article started by saying, "Following two months of frightening his bride of half a year, in an attempt to regain the affection he believed he had lost after she became an expectant mother, James Townsend shot and killed her at 9:30 Thursday night." The article went on to say, "Although he first declared the shooting was accidental, Townsend, interrogated by state police, finally admitted his wife had become cool towards him and that in order to 'drive her closer to me, I kept scaring her.'"

He told troopers he had gone out early Thursday morning and hammered away the lock and splintered the door on the tool shed to make it appear that someone was on the property. He said he did it because he meant to scare her again. "That evening while she was taking a bath in the tub in the kitchen, she told me she thought she heard someone outside. I got my rifle and went out and fired a shot. I came back in the kitchen. As I was going in the other room, I turned around and looked at her. I remember how she didn't want me near her. I remember that she had cheated on me before we were married. I cocked the rifle and drew a dead bead on her."

On November 14, 1947, the *Pittsburgh Press* reported that "a bullet from a heavy deer rifle had struck her in the jaw, piercing the brain." On Monday, November 17, the *Pittsburgh Post Gazette* stated, "The shooting occurred just as Mrs. Townsend was finishing her bath in a washtub in the kitchen of the home. She was struck in the face by the bullet and fell over dead." The *Morning Herald* of November 17 quoted Jim as stating, "I intended to shoot just past her head or nip her in the shoulder. I was so nervous I could hardly hold the gun. I did not intend to kill her, as I loved her."

In further recalling the murder to the prosecutor, Jim said, "After the gun went off I rushed over to her and yelled,

'Alice, please talk to me.' But she didn't talk. Then I ran for help. I had been drinking, but all of a sudden I was stone sober. I rushed around and tried to make it look as though someone else did it. I broke some windows and messed things up and shot at the house. I wasn't even thinking. But then I thought, 'They are going to test the rifle bullets and find that they all came from the same rifle.' I didn't know what to do."

Jim ran to get his neighbor, but what he didn't know was that this man was a former state policeman. He took one look at Jim and sensed that something was not right. Jim took off, but didn't get too far. The neighbor had called the police and they came after him, surrounding him along a stone ledge not far from his house. "By this time I really didn't care," Jim said. "I never took a life before. I don't care what anyone sez, that jars you!" They took him to the county jail in Uniontown where he remained until the arraignment.

"That's it. That's the story," Jim said. He slumped in his seat. He desperately wanted the arraignment to be over. He didn't care what happened to him; he simply wanted the inner turmoil to stop. On January 30, 1948, he appeared before the judge for sentencing. He was found guilty of first-degree murder. On January 31, the headline in *The Pittsburgh Press* read, "Wife Slayer Gets Life Sentence." The article went on to mention Jim's previous record of sex offenses. It quoted Judge Cotton who scorned state authorities for permitting Townsend's release from a reform school after he had been branded by psychiatrists as a dangerous sex offender. Judge Cotton later told Jim, "You should never get out of prison again."

After sentencing, Jim was returned to his cell. That was the last thing he remembered until the next day. The trial, the determining factor for the rest of his life, was over, and the demands of his body for rest set in. He fell asleep. When he awoke, the guard told him that he had slept for sixteen hours.

The next day Jim was taken by car to Western Penitentiary in Pittsburgh. He was handcuffed with a chain that was attached to a belt. He had no chains on his ankles. There were three people with him in the car: two in the front seat, the driver and another officer next to him, and an officer next to Jim in the back seat. Jim recalled that when he got out of the car he turned and faced the big metal doors of the prison. They opened up and he walked through them. He thought, *Oh, well.*

The doors that slammed behind him with such a deafening, clanging finality locked him in prison for the murder of his wife. They also brought to a close the first part of his life, a life of violence and abuse, fear and survival, abandonment and aloneness. As he walked through those doors, all he could see was a dead end. He wished that he were dead.

He was twenty years old.

A PRISONER OF ABUSE

CHAPTER 1

The Early Years

The stock market had crashed and the destructiveness of the Great Depression was being felt in the depths of American lives. Money was scarce and breadwinners worked wherever and whenever possible, many times at great distances from the families they were supporting. Little opportunity was available for the kind of nurturing their spouses and children needed. There were days in American families when parents had food only for their children or, for that matter, no food at all. The Townsend family was no stranger to the same stresses that affected the rest of the country at that time.

Jim was born on January 27, 1927, in Bristol, Pennsylvania, a small town northeast of Philadelphia. His father, Patrick Townsend, owned a seventeen-room house and a small coal mine, and he had $36,000 in the bank. By the time Jim was three years of age, the family had lost their mine and their money. His father soon became a bitter man. He never again had a bank account, choosing instead to stuff money in drawers or under mattresses.

During and after the Depression, Patrick Townsend worked hard at a variety of jobs. He was a miner and then a house painter. He did construction work and he even worked on a farm. He routinely put in ten- or twelve-hour days. But money was always tight, and he never had much to show for his hard work. In addition, he had to raise his five children pretty much alone because his wife was chronically ill and bedridden most of the time. Drinking was his escape and eventually he became an alcoholic. Jim called him a "meanaholic." The long hours, hard work, alcohol, and lack of money created a bitterness and hostility in Patrick that was vented on the children.

Whippings were a daily part of Jim's life. He remembered one day when, after a particularly severe beating, his father said, "I do this 'cause I want ya to be tough, so when ya git out in the world, you can take care of yourself." Well, Jim became tough all right, but in the wrong ways. He learned to use guns and knives. He learned how to lie and steal and fight. He became tough in another way too that was more subtle. In order to protect himself from the physical and emotional pain he experienced as a child, he began to stop feeling.

Jim had little support or protection on which he could depend. Because of her physical condition, his mother was powerless to stand up to his father or to nurture her children. Catherine Hawkene Townsend, Kit to his father, spent most of her time in a bed in the downstairs parlor of their home. "I never knew her to be well," was his remembrance of his mother. "When I came home from school she was always in bed."

He remembered the doctor always being there. He hated this because the doctor used to close all the windows and fill up a bowl with something that resembled tobacco or Postum. Jim never knew what it was, but it would make a lot of smoke. The smoke would break through the congestion so she could breathe. All he could think of was the doctor and the smoke and his mother hacking away. As Jim often said, "She would bring up all that stuff out of her lungs. She had more than asthma, I know, but nobody told me nothin'." The doctor's routine used to scare Jim. He thought he was hurting his mother. In his fear he would get mad at his father who didn't seem to be bothered by the doctor's treatment. Instead of understanding Jim's fears and comforting him, his father would yell, "Aw, shut up. Get the hell outside!"

In addition to Jim, there were four other children in the family: Marie, Ann, Francis, and Bob. As the oldest, Marie fit in where she was needed in watching over the family. His sister Ann, brother Francis (when he was around), and Jim did the other chores. "I was always the one who had to clean the big stove and chop and bring in the wood," Jim remembered. Francis would disappear sometimes, off working somewhere else. Later he was in the CCC (Civilian Conservation Corps).

Jim was always fighting with his younger brother, Bob. Jim was jealous of Bob at times because he really believed that Bob always got everything he wanted. In a conversation with Marie following one of his many fights with him, Jim said, "Ya know, Bob can do anything. He has a lot of talents that I wish I had. The other day he found a pair of roller skates and before sundown he was skatin'. I tried it and near killed myself. He has a way about him. Some are sayin' he has that kinda cute look. The nuns in school say, 'He's adorable.' What really makes me so mad is when Dad favors Bob in some way. Remember last week when we got into a fight and I whaled the life out of him? When I came home, Dad whaled me and asked, 'Why are you always pickin' on your brother?' You remember that for supper that night, even though we didn't have much, we had cake because of that government surplus flour we get. I got a piece, yeah, but Bob got a strawberry or somethin' special on top of his. It makes me real mad. Bob stuck out his tongue at me, as if to say, 'Nea, nea, nea.' I hate him."

There was always conflict in the Townsend home. For example, the four youngest of the children had to sleep in the same bed. Jim was always on the outside, holding on. One day Jim complained to his father, who told him to sleep at the foot of the bed. Then the other three, while moving in their sleep, would kick Jim throughout the night. One day Jim told Marie, "I just got a blanket and made a nice little place for myself beside of the bed. Doggone it, the next day Bob complained to everyone, 'How come Jim gets to sleep in a special place?' When I tried to say, 'That was mine. I made it all by myself,' Dad yelled at me, 'Jim, get back into that bed.'" When their father wasn't looking, Bob would again "rub it in" by sticking out his tongue. Jim thought, *I hate you, Bob! I hate you! There is nothin' I'd like better to do right now than grind your rotten pig face into the ground!* It was at times such as this, when his father was out of earshot, that Jim's rage spewed forth in cursing, his whole body stiffening and his white-knuckled fists ready to attack. Even at this early age, a rage was building in Jim'because he and his frustrations were not being heard.

He had learned to curse from his father, of course. This is the way it happened. One day he came into the house and said to his wife, "Kit, I'm going to kick that b-st--d to hell and back." So Jim went out on the porch to see the man his father had been talking about. His father called to Jim but got no response. When Jim finally came in, his father said, "What were you doing?" Presuming that the curse was the man's name, Jim, as a naive six-year-old, replied, "I was watchin' the b-st--d." With that, his father got the strap and started beating Jim, yelling, "You don't use that name!" Jim was confused. He was feeling, *Make up your mind what you're gonna call him. I don't understand why you can call him that and I can't.*

At times like this Jim had a lot of mixed feelings. It felt as if there was an ongoing mass inside him simmering all the time. Anger and rage at Bob were always near the surface because of Bob's ability to turn his father against him. Bob could manipulate his father in ways Jim couldn't. In Jim's eyes, Bob got what every kid has the right to have—protection and concern from his dad. He never recalled a time when he felt that his father took the time to hear him and understand his feelings. *I hate my dad for rejectin' me,* was his internal reaction.

When Jim was eight years of age, he was sent away, and his family life as he knew it changed drastically. It marked the beginning of a new life of delinquency. Jim had been getting into trouble for some time, breaking into places, stealing, and getting into fights. One night there was a group of kids together, and Jim pulled the fire alarm box. The firemen cruised street after street, and of course there was no fire. One kid, however, "ratted" on him. The police came and took Jim to the station where he was booked as an "incorrigible delinquent." For both the police and Jim's father, this incident was the last straw. He was sent to a reform school, Ellwood on the Lake, in Erie, Pennsylvania.

Ellwood was a big house with two dormitories, a large dining room, a kitchen, and a recreation room. Jim attended school but was beaten whenever he failed to get an "A," which was most of the time. He felt stupid and had to listen to the laughter and taunts of the older kids, which made him act out all the more. However, he felt positive about the people in charge, except for one lady. One day she refused to give Jim his supper because he came in forty-five minutes after they stopped serving. But the reason he didn't get in on time was that he had been working out in the barn with another kid, moving hay. The supervisors had forgotten to come get them, and when the boys walked into the house, she refused to feed them. The boys were very upset, but she wouldn't listen and she smacked Jim in the face. He got up and walked out and ran into the superintendent. Jim told him what had happened. "It's not fair," Jim said. So the superintendent went in and straightened it out. It was the first time that anyone had ever interceded on Jim's behalf.

Jim remembers being scared much of the time. He was only eight years old. He was scared that he'd get lost and nobody would find him. He was scared about what was going to happen to him. He figured that nobody wanted him and that the reason he was at Ellwood was not because he had done something bad, but because his father didn't want him at home. He doesn't remember anyone's trying to get him released, and no one ever came to see him. *Will I live here forever?* he wondered. *Will I die here?* Jim spent eighteen months at Ellwood on the Lake before returning home.

Jim returned to Bristol in 1937 to find his mother still sick. He remembered only one or two occasions when she was ever out of bed. He did, however, begin to sense that she loved him. Having reentered the public school system, he'd bring papers and other things home and she'd save them. She spent time talking to him. As difficult as it was for her, she would try and be a buffer between Jim and his dad. Jim was always concerned about her well-being and still would get angry when the doctor would do things that Jim thought hurt her. Again he didn't understand what was happening and no one explained it to him. His sister Marie was also like a mother, and Jim turned to her more frequently now.

Jim was twelve years old when his mother died. He was in great distress and felt that he could have been a better son. But he also felt that in a way she had abandoned him. *Why did she have to die now? Why did she leave me?* he questioned. At her wake he thought, *Everybody is sayin' how sorry they are and huggin' me and all that kind of stuff, tryin' to help me. Where were they before? Mom, you're gone. What am I gonna do now?*

Things changed after Kit died. Through her chronic illness, she had never been physically or emotionally able to provide a consistent nurturing presence in the daily lives of her children. With the passing of their mother, Marie took over. She made sure meals were prepared on time, laundry was done, and chores were completed. She imposed discipline when needed, for Jim and Bob a daily necessity. But Jim often said, "When you saw Marie comin' with the hairbrush in her hand, you'd better get outta there!" Marie provided an authoritative presence of steel, but also of velvet, a great contrast to their father whose harshness seemed to always dominate. Marie's consistent style of discipline and accountability, plus love and understanding, was a long time in coming to the Townsend household. It gave Jim a sense of being supported, cared for, and even loved, things he desperately needed and unconsciously longed for all of his life. Then, all of a sudden, these comforts were taken away when their father sent Marie and their reclusive sister Ann to live with and work for another family. Pat Townsend felt that he could take care of the younger children himself and also needed the income the older girls could provide. This move was a great loss for Jim. He felt a bond with Marie and he missed her.

There were, however, some positive changes that began to take place. All the medical bills were finally paid, they got electricity for the first time, and then they got a radio. Getting that radio was the most important thing that happened to Jim at that time in his life. In spite of all the fears he had from losing his mother and then Marie, in spite of his dad's anger and drinking, in spite of the fights with Bob and all the problems they had with each other, Jim looked forward to Sunday afternoon because, for some reason, they always sat together and listened to the Philadelphia Symphony. Jim often thought, *I don't know what they are gettin' out of it, but I know that I don't ever want to miss this program.*

Jim never saw much beauty nor could he describe beauty, but somehow he knew that this music was beautiful. It got into places in his insides that he didn't know were there. The music somehow talked to those parts of him. He pictured someone loving him and good things happening to him. When the music ended, he'd lose the connection with those places until the next time. But he got to know names like Tchaikovsky and Rachmaninoff. He couldn't even pronounce their names, but he got to know some of the music they wrote.

This good experience didn't last long, however, for once again Jim was sent away. He knew beforehand that there was something wrong. One Friday his brother Bob suggested that they ask their father if they could go to the movies. Movies were about fifty cents. Their father gave them each three dollars. He said, "Go to the movies tonight and tomorrow night and maybe even Sunday!" Jim thought to himself, *There's somethin' not right here.*

He wasn't even told! Monday morning when he got up, his father said "Get your good clothes on. We're gonna see some people." His brother Bob thought he knew what was happening and had already told Jim, "You're gonna go with Aunt Kit." They both liked Aunt Kit, who shared their mother's name, but instead of going to her house, Jim was sent to Saint Francis Orphanage in Essington, Pennsylvania. With no one to help raise the younger boys, Mr. Townsend had decided to put them into group homes. But in typical fashion, he never explained his decision, at least to Jim. He gave his son a hug and a kiss and then left him at Saint

Francis. Jim thought, *That's it! No explanation, no nothin'. Here I am left to myself. It feels like the time that big kid hit me in the stomach and knocked the wind outta me. You rotten little b-st--d, Bob! How'd ya do it? How come our dad goes to you to talk about me, or to tell you what is gonna happen to me? Why do you guys leave me out of it altogether? Hey, Pat, how come you don't put Bob in here too?* Jim later found out that Bob was sent to another place, Sacred Heart in Bethlehem, Pennsylvania, a better facility than Saint Francis. Jim didn't know if Bob had known ahead that he was going there or if he was just sent there, as Jim had been. He did know, however, that it was a better facility.

Saint Francis was a Catholic institution run by the Christian Brothers. It was a big house divided into a first and second division. The first division was for kids fifteen and under, and the second division for kids over fifteen. The Christian Brothers wore long black robes with a big white bib in the front and a black belt around the waist. Their faces were as forbidding and severe as their habits. When one very large, rotund brother took Jim over to Division One to get him some clothes, a vision flashed in front of him, a vision of some people taking a dog to the pound because they couldn't afford to keep it anymore. Instantly Jim knew how that dog must have felt. There he stood, alone and vulnerable, with everyone looking at him.

The Christian Brothers running the orphanage were supposed to be great educators but Jim saw them as great "whippers." He looked at them as though they were the Gestapo. They were tough. Two or three evenings a week they would have a line-up. The students had to get in line and one at a time go in and see the principal who had the student's record before him. He would peer over his glasses and say, "I see here you did this and that." Then punishment would follow. It revolved around Tasty Cakes. These cup-cakes would be passed out on Saturday afternoon. The good students got a box of them. The number of Tasty Cakes one received was dependent upon how good one's record was. Jim ended up many times with no cakes at all.

The routine at the orphanage was the same every day except for Sundays and holidays. The day started with morning Mass, then breakfast, and then study hall. After study hall there was a break, and then classes. Saturday morning was the general clean-up day. All the sheets were changed, and everyone went around the big concrete yard picking up papers. Then they had to sweep it. During the week everyone had jobs—in the kitchen, dining room, and dormitories. Despite the circumstances, Jim was actually positive about the school at the orphanage. Because they had different teachers for different subjects, he didn't get bored. Different people had different ways of teaching and he liked that. The thing he didn't like was going to Mass all the time. You had to stand, kneel, sit, do this, do that. You had to remember the catechism or get yelled at, and he was always getting yelled at. Everyone was so strict.

While he was positive about the school, there were other things building up in him that weren't, especially because he felt his father had put him there to get him out of the way. Jim was scared of the Christian Brothers. They looked so mean and menacing. There was also a bully of a kid who bothered him. For example, for lunch each boy got a little bottle of milk, a sandwich, and maybe a cookie, or a Tasty Cake cut into little pieces. One day the bully said, "Give me your sandwich." Nobody did that to Jim! As little as he was, no one messed with him the second time! The bully and Jim got into a confrontation. Jim gave him the milk all right. He poured it over his head!

But Brother Tom, in his big black robe, came to Jim and said, "Who do you think you are? What did you do that for?" Jim thought, *I didn't start it, you know, but that's life. I will never "rat" on anyone.* Part of Jim's philosophy was that you don't say anything. But before he had a chance to defend himself, the bully stated, "All I did was ask if you wanted to trade...." Brother Tom believed him and everyone made fun of Jim.

At that time Jim didn't understand it, but one of the boys was a homosexual. Jim told another kid, "There's somethin' not right about this guy. The way he acts, the funny way he talks, and all that kind of stuff." One of the guys started making fun of Jim, "You ought to stay with him. You two make a good pair."

When Jim found out what this was all about, he didn't want anything to do with him. The guys would make fun of Jim, another fight would begin, and he would again be in line to report to the principal to be punished. There were lines for other purposes too. Whenever you went to the dining hall or recreation area, there were lines for those who didn't pass tests or who got into trouble. Jim learned his multiplication tables by standing in line after flunking a math test. One day when in line, Jim thought, *I can't do this no more.*

One night at a movie, one of the guys pushed Jim out of his seat. Jim pushed him back. One of the brothers saw him and shouted, "Off to your room." Just before this incident Jim saw one of the brothers counting money. After he had finished, he lifted up the desk top and put the money away. At first Jim didn't pay any attention to it, but after he was sent him to his room, he remembered the money.

"That night about two in the morning," Jim told the officer later, "I went downstairs. The desk was locked. I figured the only way to get into it was to give it a good kick. The desktop shattered! I took the money and left. I spent about twenty bucks on food, but I guess the state police had been notified and were on the lookout for a runaway. I shot across the tracks, and there they were. I just took a step and an officer had me by the cuff of the neck. I was quickly shoved in the back of the car, which was like a cage. They took me down to the police station to the jail and then brought in my father." The school told his dad they didn't want Jim back. They said he didn't do his work and had an "uncooperative attitude," so his father took him home. He had been at Saint Francis about four or five months.

CHAPTER 2

Adolescence

J im was now back home in Bristol, and more and more he liked to be by himself. He couldn't handle the confrontations and questions from teachers, authorities, and kids about where he had been. The kids taunted him, and he kept getting into fights. He also began to experience the onset of puberty and, of course, no one had prepared him for the sensations he was feeling and the strange new experiences that looked like he had wet the bed. There was no one in the family with whom he could talk, and he couldn't risk a beating from his father, which he was sure would happen. He was convinced there was something wrong with him. He was scared, isolated, and confused.

To add to his shame and confusion, sometimes when he was asked to stand in front of the class in his Catholic school, he found himself getting aroused, which he could not control. He tried to hide it with a book or sweater, but all of his efforts seemed to call more attention to the problem. To add to his embarrassment, one of the nuns, having witnessed Jim's struggles, called him aside after class one day and explained to him what was happening in his physical development. He felt angry, embarrassed, and put down because, he thought, *I was supposed to know all about this already and not have to have some woman tell me—and a nun at that!*

Even after the explanation, Jim remained confused and scared. His teacher had told him about his physical development, but he didn't recall that she talked to him about sex. Possibly she did, but he was too overwhelmed to hear it. In the middle of these new experiences, he picked up a part-time job in a cider mill. Working there was a teenage girl with whom he got acquainted and, as he later said, "One thing led to another and we had sex." Neither of them had much information, but the experience and the exciting feelings it produced both scared them and made them desirous of more contact. At this time he also discovered masturbation, but because of everything that was going on in his world—the pressures and isolation, his fears and confusion—he put a lid on his sexual activity for a while.

More and more Jim stopped going to school. He got tired of the fighting, the taunts, and the embarrassment of dealing with the changes in his body. One day he thought, *Ya know, Jim, we can't deal with this no more!* Then he just stopped going altogether. He was in the eighth grade at the time. His father worked long hours, and Jim was left to fend for himself. There was no other adult supervision. At first he had hideouts where he could be alone. Then he got an idea. What would it be like to hop on one of the freight trains that he saw passing through town every day? He longed for more freedom and thought that riding the trains would be an exhilarating adventure.

How great it was to just take off and have all that freedom! He'd just get on a freight and go, and then get on another freight and come back. He'd come home and couldn't tell you where he'd been half the time. He wound up in all sorts of places. He knew he'd gotten as far as Texas one time, but most of the time all he knew was that he either went north, south, east, or west. When he rode the trains, he would always carry navy beans, potatoes, and other food items. Then he would jump off the train and look for the fires of the hobos. When he'd come to one, he'd eat with them and often spend the night in their camps. As he went to sleep, he thought, *Dad, what a relief that you're not around.*

By then Jim had been home about a year. Bob had returned home some months earlier and their relationship did not improve. They also started getting into trouble again. The stress in the household had not changed, but now both boys had less supervision than ever before. One day Jim suddenly found himself framed. Somebody was pulling the fire alarm boxes, and the authorities were saying, "One of these days we'll catch up with you, whoever you are." Well, Jim's brother Bob had pulled the fire alarm. When the fire company arrived, Bob said, "The guys are down yonder!" Jim was the one "down yonder," and when the fire company found him, they said, "We should have known!" Jim didn't know what they were talking about and said, "I don't know nothin'. I didn't do nothin'." They took him to the police station where he was told he was going to Glen Mills, another institution. "My father was at the station and so was my brother," Jim recounted later. "My father didn't see it, but Bob did what he always used to do—he stuck out his tongue as if to say, 'You're gone and I'm glad!'"

Jim just looked at him and said, "Someday I'll get out, and when I do, I'll beat you near to death." Jim meant it too. He was beyond anger. With his experiences of rage increasing, something almost uncontrollable was going on inside, and with all his being he wanted to come back and really hurt Bob and anyone else who hurt him again. This time he was gone for eighteen months.

The year was 1940. Jim was thirteen years old and this was the third institution he'd been in since the age of eight. Glen Mills was different, however. It was not just a reform school. You were sent there because you had committed a crime. The boys were housed in cottages run by a couple, thirty to thirty-eight boys per cottage. There were six cottages in all. There also was an administration building and a church. The cottage gave the arrangement a family-type setting, but Glen Mills was also a military school. Every day, except Sundays and holidays, the boys had military drill for at least an hour. If it rained, they drilled inside. Sunday, during the good weather, there were parades to which townspeople and other guests were invited. On Memorial Day a competition was held between cottages and the winner would receive a cup. On Sundays the Catholics went to Mass, and then everyone had to go to the Protestant church.

Everyone had a job, but Jim seemed to always wind up washing the towels. He had to do them on a washboard, and if his supervisor didn't like how they were done, Jim had to do them over again. He hated it. There were times in some of his jobs, however, when he was making the work easier without realizing it. For example, down in the coal bin, he'd move all the coal to one side, sweep out the bin, and then move the coal back. The maintenance man came down one day and said, "What are you doing?" Jim told him his procedure. "Good idea, Jim," he responded. "Keep it up." Little things like this paid off because everything was written on his record.

The emphasis at Glen Mills was on punishment, Jim concluded. If a job wasn't done right, punishment took the form of standing in a line out in the yard or standing at the dining room table to eat. This punishment might last for ten or sometimes twenty days. Standing in line also resulted from not doing the assigned schoolwork. "On line" it was called. Whenever a boy failed a test, he was written up and sent to a room where he would be whipped with a sewing machine strap. The State eventually stepped in to stop this practice. Jim used to wonder if this was the kind of thing the Nazis did in Germany. In fact, the man with the strap was called the "Nazi." Jim's back had welts from his ankles to his neck. About a year after he got out of Glen Mills, the remaining inmates attacked the "Nazi" and killed him.

The boys were rarely allowed to talk and then only outside. Silence was to be observed inside at all times. In the winter, bedtime was at 6:00 p.m. and in the summer at 6:30. In all of this routine Jim was becoming more and more volatile. His anger seethed just below the surface, and no one tried to help him deal with it or its causes. Once he ran away and lost ninety days of his time served. In other words, when a boy's monthly report was made out, he got so many check marks. If he got thirty checks, he lost thirty days. Jim would have gotten out of Glen Mills in fifteen months, but because he ran away and lost ninety days, he was there for eighteen months. At the end of that time, just prior to his release, he thought to himself, *Hey, Jimmy, what's next? Nobody's gonna help. Just keep rememberin', Jimmy takes care of Jimmy.*

But the ordeal finally was over and Jim went home again. He got a job on a farm for the summer. He rarely stood around talking or having a smoke. He worked very hard and in so doing discovered that he could get recognition and acceptance. He had had a beginning awareness of this at Glen Mills when he was doing extra work in cleaning up coal bins. At the end of the summer he got a raise to a dollar and a half a day and was made foreman of the farm. He was just fourteen years old.

As he worked hard, every now and then someone would do Jim a good turn and he'd think, *Now I've got it made.* There was a growing feeling of having some worth, but as much as he wanted to work hard at whatever he did, there was an ever-present black cloud over him that could wipe out whatever good things he had done. Out of habit he was always looking over his shoulder, waiting for something to happen that would screw it all up. He worried that his bad reputation would come back into his life and destroy the good he was trying to accomplish. He always seemed to get wiped out because of something, and he reflected upon a frequent statement he'd heard all his life: "Every time you come around, there's trouble."

Jim remembered one time working with a horse on a huckster wagon. The men would sit around in the office and play checkers and spit on the hot stove. Jim went there one day just to watch and get warm. The huckster looked at him and said, "See that nose bag that you feed the horse with? Put two cups of oats in there and take it over to my horse."

"Yes, sir," Jim saluted. "Should I give him some water too?"

"Atta boy."

He thought, *Ah ha, everything's goin' great.* After awhile he was doing little odd jobs in the office, but he always felt that something was going to happen.

One day a man started taunting the horse, which turned and severely kicked him. That wound up being Jim's fault because supposedly he had left the gate open. He said he didn't leave the gate open, wasn't even near the gate, but when he came back to the office, the owner was furious and shouted at Jim, "Get out of here and never come back."

"Give me a chance to explain," Jim begged. "I always seem to get blamed for something but am never given a chance to explain."

"Get out," shouted the owner.

Several years later Jim went back to visit his mother's grave. He ran into the man who had kicked him out and he told Jim, "You know, when I think back, you were the catchall. Anytime something happened we always came back to you. Probably by the time anything happened you just looked guilty whether you were or not, and you'd get nailed."

One day Jim's father read in the paper that they were accepting seventeen-year-olds into the Marines for the first time. The paper described how it would be done. The young recruits would go through the regular routine, but wouldn't be put into a fighting unit till they became eighteen years old—with exceptions, of course.

Jim's father looked up at him from the paper after reading this article and said, "You're seventeen, aren't you?" and nodded his own head up and down. Jim said "Yeah," even though he was only fourteen. He decided that, not knowing what his father was up to, agreeing with him was the best thing to do. The next thing he knew, he was down at the recruiting station, signed up. *Sent away again,* Jim thought.

Everything went pretty well for Jim in the Marines until he had a run-in with what they called a "ninety-day wonder." These were enlisted men who were given a ninety-day officers' training course to become second lieutenants. One day, provoked by Jim, one of these officers-in-training slapped him. Following this incident Jim explained to a hostile sergeant, "I couldn't stand being slapped so I hit him back. From all them years of being kicked around, when someone hits me, I hit him right back. Nobody slaps me without gettin' an immediate response." Jim quickly discovered that you don't do that in the Marines!

Because of this incident Jim was up for court martial. When they found out he was fourteen, they called him into the office and told him he was lucky. The colonel said, "Soldier, if you weren't under age, I would have sent you to prison, and you wouldn't have gotten out till the next century." When they escorted Jim to the bus station, one of the men told him that he'd gotten an "undesirable discharge." The man said, "If you go out there and keep your nose clean and get yourself an education, you could rejoin and make this up. You'd be surprised how far you'd go." That never happened. Where Jim eventually went had a barbed-wire fence around it with gun towers and guards. In looking back, Jim realized that if he could have stayed in the Marines, it might have been good for him because he liked the way life seemed to be held together in a disciplined, orderly way. But it didn't work out. Once again he was sent home.

In the Marines Jim had structure, routine, and discipline. Now he had none of those things, and the change was not good for him. At Glen Mills, Jim learned that working hard and doing a good job brought affirmation. The same kind of awareness continued after Glen Mills while working on the farm. Monetary reward came, along with verbal affirmation. And the Marines had provided a very disciplined context for daily life. But all of these experiences were not enough to overcome a lifetime of little self-discipline, little self-esteem, and little sense of a meaning and purpose for his life. Now, out of the Marines, he was free to do as he pleased.

After Jim was discharged, he went home to Bristol to live with his father, who had moved from the old home and was now boarding with a family named Lippencott in another part of town. Jim was fifteen years old at the time of his discharge and once again did not go back to school. Instead he became a truckers' helper. He had a little room upstairs in the Lippencott's house. For rent he cleaned the yard and the chicken coop.

Life in Bristol was a disaster. "One thing is always leadin' to another," he kept saying to himself. One day he was down at the railroad station and saw men loading boxes onto railroad cars. The boxes contained Florsheim shoes.

Jim had an idea. His stream of consciousness was always filled with ideas upon which he would act impulsively and which later turned sour. That day he told his buddy, "Hey, I know how we can get ourselves a bunch of boxes of shoes." When told where the boxes were, his buddy said, "Man, I'm not going to ride any railroad car!" Jim replied, "I'll take care of the car. I know how to ride 'em."

Jim jumped on the train as it pulled out. Just outside Bristol he opened the door of the car and pushed out all the boxes of shoes. Then he jumped off the train. His buddy was waiting with the truck. It was only then they discovered that the boxes contained only shoes for the left foot. The company always shipped the right shoes in one boxcar and the left shoes in another. Jim ended up paying his buddy gas money for the wasted trip.

"I wanted to have some fun," Jim said, "so I called the train station and told them where they could find the shoes. There was even a little piece in the newspaper about the thieves getting a shock when they discovered all the shoes were for the left foot!"

It was not surprising that Jim did not last long back in Bristol. But the offense that resulted in his being sent to a juvenile detention center in Camp Hill, Pennsylvania, was his most serious to date. The Lippencott's daughter, Marie, older than Jim, used to tease him unmercifully for not going to school. He kept hearing from Marie all the time that she was superior and he was a dummy. *Every time I'm with you, you shame me for not goin' to school. How do you get under my craw and make me feel like nothin' all the time?* he said to himself.

With these feelings the developing behavior pattern of rage rose up in Jim and finally took charge. He was angry all the time and would let things build up to a boiling point and then he would suddenly explode. Marie often was the recipient of this anger. Later he told the lawyer, "I had had enough of Marie and in a complete rage I grabbed her and beat her up and tried to force her to have sex. All of this resulted in a charge of assault and battery and attempted rape." As a result, he was sent to Camp Hill, a juvenile detention center for young criminals.

"The three-million-dollar slaughter house"—that's what the well-known journalist and radio news commentator Walter Winchell called Camp Hill. Just before Jim arrived there at age fifteen, there was an attempted escape. Four or five prisoners went over the fence. One guard shot three of them while they were scaling the fence and killed one.

Camp Hill was supposed to be a juvenile facility, but there were men there in their twenties and thirties. It was very much like a prison. The first time he went out in the prison yard and looked up, he saw guards in the tower with rifles. He was scared.

When Jim first got to Camp Hill, it was like going into an army barracks. In each barracks or unit there were about fifty cells in a first and second tier. Each barrack was named after an Indian tribe—Seneca, Mohawk, and so on. When Jim arrived, they took him into the main reception room where they removed his handcuffs. Then the guard came and led him to the storeroom to get clothes. All prisoners had to remove their street clothes and put on prison garb. Then came quarantine. During this time he was evaluated by a psychologist and a social worker and given an aptitude test. In about four or five days he was assigned a job. Jim's first job was cleaning the cellblocks. Then he was assigned to the paint gang, and the man in charge was a good teacher. He took pride in teaching his crew the right way to paint. He taught Jim how to brush paint and mix paint, and Jim learned quickly. It was something that was enjoyable to him and he felt he was doing something worthwhile.

Jim was often scared during the four years he spent at Camp Hill. Part of it was because of the guards with rifles, but he got used to them. Part of it was that he kept getting into severe fights. Jim noticed that the inmates got along if they kept quiet, but he wasn't one to keep his mouth shut, especially if he was getting pushed around.

One day he was out in the yard for recreation. The prison had hired a gym master who would put them through all kinds of exercises and games. One day he stopped as some of the guys were getting mad. He said, "Hey, my job is to make you tired." Jim said, "Well, I'm tired!" That remark resulted in extra laps around the yard for everyone. Playing catch with a football or baseball was another form of exercise. As Jim explained to a guard, "Now, I'm not much of a catcher, but when that ball's comin' hard at me I duck. And this one guy, he was really layin' that ball. A couple of times I had to reach up and get it. This one time, however, I just stepped aside and it went right through the window. One of your guard buddies came over and said, 'I'm writin' you up.' And I said, 'What did I do? I didn't throw it up there.' So we both got wrote up. The other guy said to me, 'I'll get you when we get out in the yard.'" They eventually did have a fight and they both got locked up.

The last few months before he was sent home, Jim went on a detail to Cumberland, Maryland, to pack up goods for shipment overseas during the war. This was a positive experience for him because it got him out of the violence he was part of every day. The sentence for most juveniles was eighteen months to two years. Because of his behavior Jim was at Camp Hill for four years. He was nineteen years old when he was released.

CHAPTER 3

Alice Moss

It was late in the winter of 1946 when Jim left Camp Hill. Because he was strongly advised not to return to Bristol, he decided to go to Pittsburgh where his "sponsor" lived. A sponsor was Camp Hill's name for a parole officer. The winter, when the sun rarely shines in Pittsburgh, was a dreary time to reenter the streets, and Jim had no relationships he could count on. He lived in a halfway house with other men, but basically was a loner. He was free on parole and eager to make a new start.

With the help of his sponsor he found a job with Freyvogel's, a paint store and contractor. Freyvogel's dealt exclusively in oil-based paints and began to lose money as the new latex paint, which had just come on the market, began to take hold. Jim worked there only two or three months before being laid off. Soon he found a job at Allegheny General Hospital where he started out in the laundry. Then he was transferred to the storeroom where he handed out supplies and was in charge of the inventory. One of his big jobs, first thing in the morning, was to bring down half-empty oxygen tanks from the operating room. He liked to work, he worked hard, and, as in other jobs in the past, the more affirmation he received, the more highly focused he became.

While working at Allegheny General, Jim often did odd jobs on the side. Sometimes he washed dishes in a restaurant. One time he worked for a bakery. His spontaneity and sense of humor, which had often gotten him into trouble in the past, led to mischievous pranks when things were relatively stable in his life. One day at the bakery he was told to fill the cream puffs. "Just put this end in the pastry and press a pedal with your foot and the gook goes into the cream puff," his boss told him. Jim thought he could do that. But then he ran out of "gook." As they were refilling the container, he took a piece of paper, wrote, "Sorry, we ran out," and put it in a cream puff.

Once, while working at the hospital, he was downstairs in the recreation room where the student nurses had gym classes. He was looking at a player piano and saw on the roll "Special Arrangements of Tchaikovsky's *Piano Concerto*," which had been a favorite of his when he listened to the Philadelphia Symphony on the radio as a child. He didn't see the black lady in the room who was a janitor. So he sat down at the piano, turned on the lever, and pumped the roll with his feet while moving his fingers over the keys just as though he were playing. When the roll finished, he put down the lid and got up.

"Boy, you're good," the black lady said to him.

"Thanks," Jim said, walking away.

A couple of weeks later a nurse came up to him and said, "The students are going to have a party. We would like you to come down and play a few tunes on the piano."

"Play the piano?" Jim asked.

"Yes. Dolly heard you playing and said you were good."

Jim roared. "That was a player piano. I guess I had her fooled." The nurse walked away in disgust.

During the months following his release from Camp Hill, Jim started thinking about something he had always wanted to do. He realized he had always wanted to go to the opera. *Aida* was playing in a theatre about ten miles from where he lived, so he started saving his money. He knew from looking in the society section of the newspaper that he'd have to have a tuxedo and all the trappings to look right. So he rented a tux for $18.75—that was the cost of a war bond, he remembered. He looked in the mirror and thought, *I look pretty good if I do say so myself.* He purchased a ticket and went to see *Aida*. After the opera, dressed in his tux and feeling like Rockefeller, he decided to go to a particular restaurant and have something to eat. *What about all them fish eggs,* he wondered, so he ordered caviar and a biscuit and a glass of wine. *I'm feelin' very fancy, he thought.* When he got the check, he froze. He had fifty dollars and the bill was forty-eight. He just laid the fifty-dollar bill in the little saucer and got up and left. He thought, *Now I have to walk all the way home in my tux.* The next day he was tired. *I really had a great time though,* he thought. *Maybe all them years of being locked up made me want to have experiences like this.*

Life was good for Jim in these early months. There were new experiences and spaces of time where things didn't seem so heavy. *I wasn't lookin' over my shoulder all the time to be sure I'd be OK. It would be great if this kind of life could continue,* were lingering thoughts.

While Jim was working at Allegheny General Hospital, he became part of a small gang of guys and girls who met in the woods not far from a local park. Two people were in charge of this gang: "Big Dad" and "Mom." Big Dad was big-boned and had a weather-beaten face that always needed a shave. He had deep lines around his mouth and had hands that looked as big as a baseball mitt. In charge of the girls was Mom. Mom was a huge six-footer who towered over everyone and who could knock anyone across the room with one swipe of her hand. Jim kept wondering what Big Dad and Mom's marriage was like.

This gang had one objective—sex. Each time they met, everyone would sit in two rows, the girls on one side and the guys on the other. They would start bidding to see who would be their sexual partner that night. If a girl wanted to bid on a guy, she did, or vice-versa. The guy or the girl then went to the highest bidder, and then off they would go into the woods. When he was first introduced to this gang, Jim was "bid on" by Judy, a girl with a reputation of being "the best." Perhaps it was their mutual arrogance that attracted them to each other. Perhaps Judy just wanted to try out the new guy. At any rate, she won Jim and was ready to go off into the woods like the other couples were doing, but Jim just wanted to sit around and drink his beer. Finally Judy said, "When are we goin'?"

"What do you mean?" Jim answered. He still wasn't sure of the routine.

"Well, you know, let's get it on!"

"I don't want to do nothin' now. I just want to drink my beer."

With that Judy swung at him and hit him in the face. He hit back instantly, breaking her jaw. Judy screamed and swore, running to "Mom" in a fury of anger and pain. Soon Mom appeared. She stood up next to Jim and leered, "Why don't you smack me?" Although Jim was lean and just five feet seven and a half, an aggressive opponent generally did not intimidate him, no matter how big. He hauled off and swung. He threw a fist. After that, all he felt was searing pain. He landed on his back and Mom's foot was on his chest as she said, "There's nothin' big about you." And she was right. Jim had been reduced to nothing—again. Then, taking her foot off his chest, she picked him up and dragged him to her tent. "I like a dog like you," she said. "I'm gonna teach you how to treat a woman." That night Jim's humiliation and degradation deepened. Mom had complete control over him and made him feel like nothing. He learned more about sex and women that night than he ever had before, but many of the things he learned haunted him for years. He felt like an animal. He had experienced deep humiliation and, on top of that, he suffered a beating at the hands of a woman. But he continued with the gang because he was hooked on sex. He wasn't scared like he used to be. He knew that he was good at it and felt like he could get a woman to want him. Time after time he did.

After he had been in the gang about a month and a half, he met Alice Moss, a new employee at the hospital where he worked. As soon as he met her, he started trying to get her to have sex with him, but Alice was different from the other girls. She wanted to remain a virgin until she was married, and Jim definitely wasn't interested in marriage. But he liked Alice and thought that if he got her into the gang, he could wear her down and get what he wanted. So he asked a girl in the gang to get close to Alice and to tell her that this group— this gang—had a lot of fun together. She never mentioned the way they had fun, so one night Alice came. As was the custom, they lined up, guys on one side and girls on the other, and started the bidding. Jim really wanted her so he started the bidding at twenty dollars. Then Judy (the girl whose jaw he had broken) said, "And twenty-five cents." No matter what Jim bid, Judy would add twenty-five cents to his price. They got up to over one hundred dollars, but eventually Jim saw that he would never win so he stopped bidding.

Judy sauntered over to him and taunted, "You really want her, don't you?"

"Yeah," he replied.

Judy wanted to get even. She had not forgotten his attack on her and his subsequent "big night" with Mom. Judy said, "If you want her, I'll make you a deal. You go out with her and in thirty days, or ninety at the most, get her to agree to marry you."

Jim was still looking for gang acceptance. Judy had challenged him in front of other members of the gang and he could not lose face. Pride would not let him back down—not to Judy! So he agreed.

He pursued Alice but she never returned to the gang again. They went to movies and restaurants, he learned to pull out the chair for her at tables, he opened the door for her, and he got dressed up a lot. He had never done those things before. He began talking to her, really talking. He had never before talked so much to one girl, and he never touched her or even tried to. How come? he thought. After awhile all he could think of was that he might lose her and that drove him crazy.

They liked to take long walks and go swimming. She loved nature. She knew many different areas in Pittsburgh, and they'd get on a trolley and go all over town. Then they'd go up to the top of a hill at night and look over the city and its lights. She loved music and she was always surprised that he liked classical music. She used to laugh and say, "You can't even pronounce the names of these composers." He laughed back. She was right, of course, but he loved the music and they listened to it together.

They got to know each other. Jim had never taken the time to get to know anyone. Girls were for sex, that was all, but he loved being with Alice. She always smelled so good and she had long, beautiful hair, which he loved. He loved watching the men look at her and whistle. It made him feel proud that she was his girl.

One day, after three months, he finally said, "You know, Alice, I think we get along pretty good. We don't want much in life and all that. I was just wonderin' if you'd like to get married."

"I was just wonderin' how long it was gonna take you to ask," was her reply.

Jim went, "Phew!"

The original deal was that Jim would then go to Judy and say that Alice had said "Yes," not giving a hoot about Alice. Instead, when he went to Judy, he said, "I want you to meet my woman. She's titled. She's mine. We're engaged." As he said to a friend, "Love just sort of snuck up on me without me realizing it was happening." Yes, he still was having sex with other girls. Alice heard about that, but he convinced her it wasn't true. He didn't understand the big deal. Sex was sex, but with Alice it was love.

Jim and Alice were married on May 10, 1947, in a small Methodist church in a suburb of Pittsburgh. At that time they were living in separate rooms in the same rooming house. The landlady and her husband were their witnesses and only guests. They took the newly married couple out to lunch after the ceremony. Jim hated suits but he wore one to his wedding. Alice wore a coral dress with a black and white striped jacket and white shoes. To Jim she was the most beautiful creature he'd ever seen. They had no honeymoon. Alice just moved into his room. He learned just how much a woman could save as Alice arrived with box after box of stuff, but soon she put her imprint on the place. They didn't stay there long, however, because the landlords were selling the house. By luck the house right across the street from Allegheny General Hospital had an apartment on the first floor. There was a bedroom, small kitchen and bath, and a combination living/dining room. The price was pretty good, so they moved in, and Alice made that place home.

Alice and Jim started to live life as a married couple. They attended church and participated in various activities—dances, picnics, and concerts. They continued to listen to the Philadelphia Orchestra on the radio every Sunday afternoon. They loved music and their happiest times revolved around music. Alice took good care of her new husband and enjoyed housekeeping—cooking, baking, sewing, decorating their tiny apartment.

One day Jim bought her a dress. It was black with sequins on it. He told a friend, "When she puts that dress on, unless you're blind, you know you're lookin' at a woman. Wow! I got this dress for her because it was her. I don't know nothin' about clothes, but when I seen that, I said, 'Boy, I bet she'd look…you know….' I always liked her in that dress. Of course, then I had to go out and borrow money from different people to buy a necklace and bracelet to go with the dress.

"One day I came home and told her we were goin' to a party—a real formal affair and I said, 'Wear your dress.' Prior to this event I had to stop at Woolworth's for somethin' and I seen this bracelet that had a cup, plate, knife, fork, and spoon, and a chop of some sort on it. I think there was a glass too. I think they call them charm bracelets. It only cost $2.39, including tax!

"When I got home, I said, 'Here, I thought this'd look nice on you,' She made a big fuss over it and all that stuff, and I'm figuring, 'What the hell, I spent more on the other jewelry and she wasn't as excited.'

"But this day of the party, when she came out wearing the dress that I liked so much, the only jewelry she was wearing was that charm bracelet. I said, 'Why do you got that on?' And she said, 'You are my food and drink.' I thought, *This girl is weird.*"

That incident kept coming to Jim's mind as he really began to see what love was all about. It was little things like the bracelet that brought out Alice's smile. She was beautiful, blonde, and blue-eyed, but it was her attitude about things that impressed Jim the most.

He remembered a time when he came home one night all messed up because of one thing or another. Alice was supposed to go out. As a matter of fact, she had been looking forward to it. She met every Tuesday with a group of women and they'd talk about "women stuff." On this occasion she decided not to go. She stayed home to make sure Jim was OK. He kept telling her to go, reminding her that she had made an agreement to be with these friends, but she said, "No." When he looked back at things like this, he realized that Alice had taught him a lot about love. But then he'd think, *You, Jim, were a piece of garbage. You were a jerk with her, even unfaithful. What the hell was the matter with me!*

Their life began to change after they had been married only a few months.

Allegheny General Hospital began layoffs, and Jim was one of the ones let go. He was on unemployment for awhile, but then he met a police officer who had a farm in Ohiopyle, Pennsylvania, fifty miles from Pittsburgh. He hired Jim to work his place and to help him start to raise cattle. Jim and Alice moved out to the farm and Alice set about making a new home for them.

At first everything was a continuous honeymoon, and Alice had him working hard to get the place in good shape. There was a creek running through the property, and Alice talked Jim into digging up little bushes and putting them along the bank. Then he raked it all and laid stones in the creek to make it bubble. She loved it. Their days were spent walking on the property and making love. It was a wonderful time. But then things began to change. Alice had become pregnant soon after they were married, and she had become distracted and preoccupied. As her pregnancy continued, Jim began to feel her pull away from him more and more. Was this happening again in his life? Once again he felt that he was being cut off from someone important to him. As he felt her pulling away, he didn't understand what was happening. He didn't understand the effect of pregnancy. A pregnant woman is not interested in sex in the middle of morning sickness or at some other fanciful time her partner may wish, or everyday, for that matter. By the time she was six-months pregnant, Jim felt he was losing her and he couldn't handle that. No one was ever going to walk away from him again, especially Alice, someone he loved so much. He was desperate. "Then—bang. It all ended."

The next day, November 14, 1947, the *Pittsburgh Press* reported that "a bullet from a heavy deer rifle had struck her in the jaw, piercing the brain." In further reporting on November 17, the *Pittsburgh Post Gazette* continued, "The shooting occurred just as Mrs. Townsend was finishing her bath in a washtub in the kitchen of their home. She was struck in the face by the bullet and fell over dead."

A Prisoner of the State

CHAPTER 4

Western Penitentiary

The moment had arrived. The ride from the Uniontown jail had just ended. Handcuffed and flanked by guards, Jim stepped out of the back of the police car. The officers in the front seat, whom Jim had seen merely as hulking forms through the metal grillwork partition, also flanked him. He walked through the gaping thick metal doors of the prison and heard them clang shut behind him. Through a blur of activity he was fingerprinted, given a uniform, photographed, and then locked in a cell. He walked through it all as a robot: mindless, withdrawn, and distracted. He remained alone in his cell for the next seven days before being allowed to enter the general prison population.

It was not a good beginning. The first day Jim went into the prison yard he got into a fight. He felt he had to set everybody straight. He was figuring that they were going to say, "Here comes a nice young guy. He's not too bad lookin'." So he thought to himself, *I gotta make it real clear that no one is gonna mess with me.* Jim went over to a large black man in the yard and, with all of his five-foot-seven-and-a-half-inch strength, hauled off and hit him in the jaw. The surprised victim picked him up and threw him to the pavement, almost killing him. The black man said to the guard, "Man, I don't know nothin' about this guy. I never seen him before!" The black man's name was Purdue, and the guards locked both men up in the "hole" where they stayed a few days. When they came out of the hole, they were separated, Jim sent to the west wing while Purdue stayed in the east wing. One day after they were allowed to return to the yard, Jim looked up to see Purdue coming toward him. He thought an attack was coming, but Purdue stopped a few feet away and said, "I gotta ask you a question, man. You don't even know me. You never saw me before in your life. What the hell did you hit me for?"

"Because I wanted everyone here to know they aren't to mess with me," Jim replied.

Purdue said, "Don't worry about that, man. Everyone here figures that you're nuts. Nobody's gonna come near you." The two men started to talk and during the weeks that followed a friendship began.

During the early months the guards and his fellow prisoners saw Jim as a madman. He also felt that way about himself. His constant thought was, *I don't care about anybody or nothin', just nobody get in my way.* His surroundings contributed to his attitude. Everything about them was oppressive. The fortress-like grayish walls, with tiers rising five stories above the main floor, provided little daylight in the cells. With the height of the walls in the yard, there was no way to see beyond the prison. He felt stifled and caged.

Jim's daily community consisted of hardened criminals, and he was considered one too. Many of these men were in prison gangs, and power struggles between them were rampant. Membership was signified in different ways. For example, rosary beads and crucifixes in various colors were used to determine which gang you were in, and also became visible instruments in provoking confrontations between gang members. Muslims would state their gang identity by wearing their caps at a particular angle. In addition to the power struggle that determined which gang was "King of the Hill," competitive sports created conflict both on and off the field. Tickets of admission for a baseball or football game or handball competition would be made out of scraps of paper. Some inmates were powerful enough to determine payment and back up their demands. Payment for tickets could be in cigarettes or whatever else was considered of value.

Stealing was rampant. One day an inmate told Jim that a guy stole his eyeglasses and demanded several packs of cigarettes to get them back. Jim told him to refuse, but the guy didn't follow Jim's advice. The inmate didn't have the guts to stand up to him and instead gave him the cigarettes. Gambling of one sort or another was a daily event. Gang rapes were a frequent occurrence, and a certain way to get beaten up was to try to move in on someone else's "boy."

Jim fit right into the violence going on around him. The months following his arrival were filled with fighting. Jim provoked many of these fights, and although some days he was very frightened, other days he was too enraged to fear anything. He instantly communicated his anger by "mouthing off" at everyone. He fought constantly, both verbally and physically, the prison system, the guards who represented and enforced it, and the inmates. His ability to get upset and react was instant. In a rage he would just begin swinging and then would be locked up along with the others involved. He was one inmate who was a constant source of disorder.

While all this was going on, there was another battle raging. What he also constantly fought but never defeated was the nightmares. Every night in his dreams, Alice would come and sit next to him with a tormented expression on her face. She would just sit and look at him. She was always holding a little child who asked, "Why, Daddy?" There was no relief from this nightly experience. His own terrified screams, which echoed throughout the cellblock, would awaken him as he tried to get his breath. Once awake, he would become aware that his body was drenched with perspiration and shivering uncontrollably. Then he would go into a rage, pound his head on the wall, and throw things around the cell. Eventually the guards had to put him in a padded cell.

Finally in desperation he went to a prison counselor for help. "These nightmares is what is real for me," he told him. "It's like I'm being torn to shreds inside, and after them dreams I become more and more violent. Even when I'm put in a padded cell, yellin' and stuff, nothin' gets these thoughts out of my mind. They just keep stickin' to me. I try beatin' them from my head with my fists or on the cell wall, but they keep comin'."

He went on to tell the counselor, "During some days I get beaten down with thoughts to put the blame on Alice for it all. I remember kickin' her dead body after the murder, yellin' that it was her fault that it happened, not mine. 'You pulled away, Alice!' I'd scream. There were feelings and moments that would beat me up. I know I'll never leave this prison!" The counselor couldn't help him. The nightmares continued.

The terror and anxiety he faced each night left him totally exhausted, and the helplessness to control his thoughts increased his anger. His anxiety increased when one day he was told that he had two visitors. *Visitors! Who? No one has ever come to see me.*

"Who is it?" Jim asked the chaplain.

"It's your father and your brother Fran." Jim froze and sat down.

"No one in the family has ever come to see me. What's this all about?" *This father of mine was glad to get me out of his hair and into the Marines. Why would he want to see me now?* Jim became aware that he was breathing more rapidly and that powerful *feelings* were starting to emerge.

As the guard, leading him with his hand on his arm, turned the corner in the hall toward the visitor's room, Jim saw his father and brother through the window in the door. Fran was sitting on his father's left at a round table. His father was sitting with a straight, rigid back in the metal visitor's chair. His cane was planted between his knees, with his hands clasped around the top of the handle. Jim wondered for a moment whether he was even breathing. His face was rugged, strong, and expressionless.

As the door opened, Jim saw his father stiffen even more. His brother stood to greet him. Pat Townsend, their father, remained seated and looked straight ahead. The guard released Jim and, with his arms folded across his chest, stood at the door while Jim, Fran, and their father sat around the table in awkward silence.

Fran began talking about the family. Eventually his father, looking just past Jim, asked, "How are you?" He never made eye contact.

"Fine," Jim replied.

"If you ever get out of here, I'm going to leave the country," were his father's next and last words. For the remainder of the allotted time he said nothing. Jim felt that he was no longer really there. By this time, the feelings that had started to emerge when he heard of his father's presence were too numerous to identify. He was almost unable to think. It felt like radio static had jammed his head, but the stiffening of his body and the realization that his fists were clenched and ready made him remember his raging experiences as a boy with Bob and his father. At this moment within himself his whole being screamed, *you rotten b-st--d crud of a father! Your silence always hurt me so bad. Did you come here just to do this to me again? Why did you come at all?*

The guard signaled that the time was up and escorted Jim out of the room. During the weeks that followed, he wrote several letters home, but they were never answered. No one ever visited him again during his thirteen-year stay at Western.

One morning he awoke trying to find some energy and motivation to be able to face the day. As he lay there, he felt that he was drowning in an increasing sea of depression. He began to reflect, *This is now my sixth year here in Western. A life sentence is still lookin' me in the face. I know that I will never get out of here. I'm done!*

Jim's mind then moved to another prisoner who kept pushing him to have sex with him. In his hopelessness, all of a sudden he thought that he was going to get this handled once and for all so this guy would never approach him again. He thought, *Ya know, I could take care of two problems here. I have no fear of killing myself. I don't care about nothin'. I'm done anyway. I'm gonna kill myself and I'm gonna take this guy with me.* Jim and this guy Jack both lived on the fifth tier at Western. Jim began to plan his strategy. *I'll arrange to meet him somehow up on this level and, holding him, quickly step up one rung of the guardrail, which will make it high enough for me to push my weight over the top of the rail. Then I'll fall five stories down into the center of the prison, taking him with me.*

Arrangements were made to meet, but Jack never showed up. His work time had been extended. Disgusted, Jim went back to his cell, got on his bunk, and fell asleep, a deep sleep with no nightmares. For the first time in months he felt rested and for the first time in months felt that he had some clarity of mind. He thought, *Killin' myself is bein' a wimp.* He decided that prison wasn't going to get him down. When the guy finally found him, Jim said, "Listen, you little f-----, you know I'm not afraid of takin' punishment for killin' you. I will do that if you don't back off as of now. I mean it." Jim knew that if Jack so much as touched him, he would have killed him. After this incident, and the decision that prison wasn't going to get the best of him, something was different in Jim. *I don't know how to describe hope,* he thought, *but I think that's what I'm feelin'. But how do ya keep it? That's what I want to know.*

And yet this new sense of hope came and went depending upon what happened each day or in what stage of depression he found himself. The hope in him was not yet strong enough to help control the depression or to help change the unresolved anger and rage of a lifetime. Fighting, both physically and verbally, still provided a sense of overcoming or doing something about those things that undermined him. For example, there were strict rules for everything including how to keep your cell. In defiance of these rules Jim created a fake altar in his cell, took a candy bar, broke it into pieces, and sprinkled the pieces on top of the altar. In the heat of the day, the pieces melted and made a strange pattern on the "altar." The guards challenged him, telling him it was against the rules. Of course, he told them what they could do with their rules! He was called to a trial in the prison to give a reason for breaking the rules and to explain what the altar and broken candy meant.

In the trial all of his anger spewed forth. As was his constant pattern, hostile, verbally profane vitriol poured out of his mouth. He made it clear that what went on in his cell was none of their business and he didn't *know* what the altar meant. The situation was bizarre enough for the authorities to question his stability, but they also realized that no amount of reason could penetrate his defiance and hostility, which kept him in open conflict with others all the time. He was sentenced to six months in the "hole."

After he was told that he was to be sent to the hole, two guards escorted him out into the prison yard and toward a brick wall containing a large double door. Guards on either side of the doors opened them as Jim and his escorts were cleared for entry. Jim had been through this process many times before. At this point he was tired and wrung out from the trial and the expenditure of so much energy from all of his anger. As he was taken to another building—a prison within the prison—he felt like a dog always being controlled by a jerking choke collar attached to a short leash.

These feelings were still roaming around his tired mind when he came to the door of the cellblock known as the "hole." After being cleared, the guards led him in. *Which cell on what tier is it gonna be this time,* he thought as he looked up at the small version of the big prison with two to three tiers of cells above him. His cell this time was on the first floor. As he entered, he noticed that nothing had changed since the last time he was in the hole. The cell had the usual small window, toilet, sink, and bunk. The walls were in the same color green.

Before they even started to tell him, he knew the daily drill. He would be locked up for twenty-three hours each day. For one hour of the day he could go out to the special yard for the cellblock. Handball could be played or other exercise done. Once a week he could take a shower and change his clothes. Meals were brought to the cell. After the evening meal and the head count, the lights were turned out. At that time something else happened. A guard would clap his hands. With this signal, the hole erupted as the prisoners began to scream and yell at the top of their lungs, either into the air or to or at each other. The one hour of exercise certainly didn't handle all of the frustrations of their confinement and boredom. The more strict confinement and silence in the hole was supposed to help them face their inner conflicts and deal with why they had been put in there. But, of course, that rarely worked because they had no tools with which to deal effectively with such things.

It was in the cooling down time of one of these screaming and yelling periods that Jim heard, "Hey, Jim, is that you sayin' all them bad words?" This question came from a buddy in a cell on the second tier above Jim's cell.

"Yeah," replied Jim. "Why do ya want to know?"

His buddy responded, "It's 'cause I got a couple of books maybe you'd like to read. I'll get 'em to you."

These books somehow found their way to Jim's cell. He flipped through some pages and then tossed the books on the floor in the corner. Jim's reading skills, along with his attention span, were limited and he had never read a book from cover to cover. He would read two or three pages and then give up, or he would turn to the last chapter and try to put the pieces together in his head.

One of the books he received was from the Tarzan series and the other was the first book of the Zane Grey series. After several weeks, with the demons in his head gaining strength and the exhaustion from terror-filled nights overwhelming him, he picked up the Tarzan book and started leafing through its pages. Then he thought, *I might as well start at the beginning and see how far I get.* To his amazement he began to find it difficult to stop reading, though he read very slowly. As the story unfolded, Jim's mind was filled with impressions and images and at times moments of identification with the tragic beginnings of this infant who would be called Tarzan. As Jim described it to Purdue when he got out of the hole, "Tarzan's parents were

in some kind of camp-like shelter near the edge of a cliff—
and somehow in a storm this camp fell over a cliff. His parents died and Tarzan, a new baby, was left there alone,
abandoned. Then a bunch of apes come along and the little
baby of one of the apes had just died. So the mother leaves
the dead baby ape and takes Tarzan. Ya know, I discovered
that Tarzan means 'white ape.' That's how he got his name."

The more Jim read, the more he realized how much he
was enjoying it. His mind started to figure, *Boy, that would
be somethin', flyin' around, hangin' at the end of a vine,
flyin' all over them branches like that, eatin' when you're
hungry, sleepin' when you're sleepy, not havin' nightmares,
havin' fun with the natives, bein' able to talk to the animals.
Wouldn't that be somethin' if you could sit down and talk to
a snake, a tiger or an ape, 'cause I bet they see a lot of things
we don't see.*

Jim continued to imagine: *I would like to be like
Tarzan—nobody tells him what to do and all that stuff.
Tarzan grew up to be strong and he had a lot of freedom. He
has a sense of humor. It's fun bein' with Tarzan when he
sneaks into the natives' huts and hides their spears and stuff
like that. This is great!*

Jim enjoyed Tarzan, but it was when he began reading
Zane Grey that he really got hooked on reading. The
descriptions of riding on a horse across the plains, what the
plains looked like, and what the heat of the day felt like
made it all come alive for him. He often stated that in reading Zane Grey he could get a suntan by just being in the
words on the page. He also was impressed when he heard
that Grey, an ex-preacher, didn't like the way the government was treating the Indians so he wrote books to bring to
the readers' attention the things that were going on. *Imagine
bein' able to write like that,* he reflected.

Jim was continually attracted to the characters in the stories. He saw himself as the guy who called his horse "Dearly Beloved." This guy, who was helping people, could outdraw anybody or throw a knife better than anybody when he was helping people. Jim saw himself as the good guy in these stories. He wanted to be the one who would go out and help the poor or the guys on the wagon trail. Reading Zane Grey reminded Jim of pictures he had seen of his father when he was a cowboy in Arizona before it became a state. His father told him he got twenty dollars a month, a lot of money in those days. He remembered stories of his father riding across vast stretches of land. Jim's thoughts had to do with freedom and the lore of the land. His love of the land had begun while he was working on the farm at Ellwood. He loved seeing things grow, which he saw daily on the farm, and he loved the forest and streams and open spaces. He remembered a lot of open spaces while riding the "freights" as well. The more he read, the more he realized, *Readin' keeps showin' me a lot of what's out there and all kinds of experiences I could have.*

Jim's six-month sentence in the hole finally came to an end, and he was released once again into the general prison population. It wasn't long before he reconnected with Purdue. Since their fight in the prison yard when Jim first entered Western, they had become friends and would always pick up where they had left off between their times in the hole. As they got to know each other better, some humor began to enter the grimness of most days.

Purdue had only one tooth in the front. He loved corn-on-the-cob but it would take him forever to eat it. This drove the guards crazy. "Why don't you cut the corn off the cob?" they asked, impatiently. Purdue would then jump up and shout, "Deputy, deputy, this man is pickin' on me."

Jim and Purdue were jogging in the yard one day while they were talking and a fellow inmate walked by and said, "How you doin', m.f.?" Purdue said, "Alright." Then another guy came up and said, "Hey, m.f., how's your m.f. mother?" He said, "Alright. She got out of the hospital and probably in another couple of weeks she's gonna come down and visit me." And he said, "Hey, great." Jim saw another guy approaching who came up and said, "Hey, you dirty m.f." Purdue, with one punch, embedded him into the pavement. Jim asked, "Why did you hit him?" Purdue answered, "I ain't dirty. These dudes need to learn how to use the right adjectives!"

Purdue and Jim did a lot together. They were assigned to work in the tailor shop. Purdue made the holes for the buttons and Jim then sewed them on. One day Jim looked at Purdue and said, "We're becoming one *hell* of a team." Working in the tailor shop was better than doing license plates. If you were assigned to the license plate shop, you just put numbers on the plates. Jim spent a lot of time there and got quite good at it. He earned sixty cents a day. If you did a certain number of plates, you got a bonus. However, it was dull, boring work. At that time the economy was going through a recession and only one license plate per car was required. This eliminated a lot of work and there were not enough other assignments to keep the prisoners busy. Prisoners who weren't working were locked up in their cells because there was not much else to do. Schooling was available, but at that time Jim didn't have much to do with it. He felt he had learned a lot in the tailor shop, but in most jobs there was little training. Whatever work he had, however, wasn't enough to block out the memories that attacked him daily following the nightly episodes of terror in reliving his murder of Alice. This went on year after year.

While Jim was continuing his work with Purdue in the tailor shop, there was a discernable unrest taking place in prisons in Pennsylvania. Western Penitentiary erupted at one point. The overcrowding and lack of work that kept the prisoners locked up much of the time bred unrest and more violence. It became clear to the authorities that the prison population had to be reduced. To try and find a solution to this problem, prison officials began to examine who might be eligible for transfer to Rockview Penitentiary in Bellfonte, Pennsylvania. Rockview was a minimum-security prison that provided better living conditions. When Jim first heard the name Rockview, he asked a buddy about it. The answer came, "Well there's a big farm they have out in the country. All they got is a fence around it." *How about that,* Jim thought.

After learning that at Rockview some of the inmates drove trucks to bring supplies back and forth, Jim became even more interested. He began to think that if he could get to Rockview and get that job as a truck driver, one trip out of the compound would be the last they would see of him. He believed he could make it work. But how could he get to Rockview? After all, he had committed a violent crime. He was serving a life sentence. He was a constant source of fighting and disruption in the prison. He had a bad reputation. Many times he had been told that if he "kept his nose clean," life would get better, but he always blew off that suggestion. When he found out that there might be a possibility of eventually getting transferred to Rockview, however, he began to plan a strategy. *Boy, I'm gonna bow and "yes sir" everybody,* he thought. *"How ya doin'?" "Fine, sir, how's yourself?" I'll say it even if it's an inmate. I'm gonna have the cleanest cell. My clothes will always be neat. I'm gonna keep myself shaved and washed. I'm gonna get a good report if it kills me. I want to get out of here! I have to get out of here!*

Another part of the strategy was that Jim began to attend Mass. *All this hocus pocus don't mean nothin'*, he thought after attending a few times. He got magazines and read in the back of the chapel during the service. He had briefly worked as a custodian in the chapel while he was still making license plates and sewing on buttons in the tailor shop. He hated being there and lamented, *This is all I need, to have to mop up and down this place. I hate watchin' these chaplains come and go in here doin' their stuff. Who cares about all this? I hate runnin' the projector for the Protestant chaplain. I hate all of them for that matter, pushin' their weight around. You're all fools believin' all this stuff with the wine and everything.* But still he attended Mass every Sunday. He thought it would look good on his record.

As soon as Jim realized the possibility of being transferred to Rockview and made a decision to change his behavior, there was an almost immediate transformation. He stopped fighting, and refused to respond to the challenges and taunts of other inmates. He cleaned himself up and kept his cell neat. He cooperated with the guards. In every way he became a model prisoner. During this time something happened that would have a lasting impact on his life. He was asked by the chaplains to come and work in their office. From his previous stint as a custodian, they knew that Jim could buff floors and do other maintenance duties. There was a lot of work taking care of floors, pews, the altar, and hymnbooks, and all of the chaplains were eager to get him. In this job he had work to do every day, unlike making license plates, which was dependent upon market demand. Working everyday kept the demons from the nightmares from devouring him by the time the day ended. His plan was, *I'm gonna do a day's work, I'm botherin' nobody, I'm only gonna take a smoke at lunch. When I finish work, I'm gonna shower and then go back to my cell.* Once in a while he'd come out into the yard, but most of the time he'd stay in his cell and read Zane Grey.

While he was lying on his bunk at night, he realized he was thinking more and more about what he was doing and seeing. Each day a lot of inmates would come into the chaplain's office sad and depressed and then go out feeling better. It happened over and over. Jim figured, *I guess it's like havin' a good shot of whiskey—it makes 'em settle down.* Many times a month, while working in the chaplain's office, Jim would be the one sent out into the yard, the scene of so many fights he had started, to give an inmate some bad news from home. He would yell out an inmate's number and then tell him his mother or wife or kid had died, or that he was being served with divorce papers, or that someone was quite ill. Jim eventually became known as the "death squad." The inmates would say, "Well, here comes the death squad again," and they'd listen for their number.

Sometime each day Jim would find himself sitting with an inmate who was waiting to meet with a chaplain. They would talk about different things—circumstances, feelings, and problems. One day many months later an inmate, who had been to the chaplain's office, came to Jim and said, "You know, I've thought of you a couple of times. I don't know how you keep your sanity, talking to everybody, and a lot of times in the yard I seen people call you names and you just say, 'Well, at least I know who I am!' You're different now. How come?" Jim just shrugged his shoulders. "I dunno," he replied.

During this time Jim was still telling the chaplains what they could do with all the "communion hocus pocus," while at the same time doing more and more in the office. Many times he would be in conversation with an inmate and then bring him into the chaplain's office saying, "Father, you ought to talk with this guy." He'd say, "Jim, that's pretty good." Jim would think, *Yeah! Just write it on my record.* Work in the chaplain's office filled Jim's days, but one day he found that he was going to be locked up every weekend for the next six weeks. He had been asked if he had seen a certain thing happening involving some other inmate. "I didn't see nothin'," Jim replied. He told them that he'd been inside the chapel at the time. The guard said, "Well, the windows were open." Jim responded sarcastically, "Well, I don't go lookin' out the windows." His old attitude was still alive in spite of his self-effort to control it, and it got him the six-week weekend sentence. Before being locked up on Friday, he had to bathe and give up his radio. He would then enter his cell where he remained until Monday before work.

These weekends became important because he had time to read. He spent hours reading *Reader's Digest, The Saturday Evening Post, Life,* and newspapers. He realized that he was staying connected to what was going on in the world, and years later when he was released from prison, he realized that all of his reading had been a good preparation for his reentry into society. The cost of food, clothing, and apartments; employment opportunities; attitudes of society toward people like himself—all these were things he learned from magazines. Reading was now something he had to have in his life.

Changes ever so quietly continued except for smoking. Then one night in his cell before lights-out Jim saw that he had time to smoke a cigarette, but he was out of matches. He called to a guard who was walking in front of his cell smoking a cigarette and asked him for a light. The guard just looked at him and walked away. Jim thought *Ya know somethin', this is the last time I'm gonna depend on anybody else for what I need. As of now I quit smokin'.* Yeah, the three packs a day and *smokin' since I was fifteen may make it tough, but every time I want to smoke I'm gonna have your pig face in front of me. Believe me, I'll find a way to be better than you, and I will never have to rely on you again for nothin'.*

The use of sugar ended as quickly as the use of cigarettes. While smoking, a lot of sugar in a cup of coffee gave an extra kick of energy and a satisfying taste. However, soon after he stopped smoking, a sugar-loaded cup of coffee one morning made him nauseated. He never used sugar in coffee again.

During this time in Western Penitentiary changes were taking place in his life that were not yet a conscious part of his understanding. Years later at Rockview he wrote in a journal his reflections about this transition time: "I didn't realize that my bad attitude was getting better and it wasn't only because I wanted to get to Rockview. I wanted to read more and more because I was learning so many new things that excited me and that I spent hours wondering about. I was also learnin' about me—who I am. Imagine me interested in learnin', havin' a goal (such as wanting to control my behavior), to get a good record so I might get to Rockview. My motives were still screwed up at that time, but I'm thinkin' there was some kind of hope and somethin' I'm to do I never seen before. I'm realizin' this was happenin' because I really wanted somethin' different!"

During those last months at Western he was obsessed with the desire to get to Rockview and get the truck job that would be his ticket to freedom. The state, with the mandate to reduce Western's population, started looking at prisoners who might be eligible for a nonmaximum security prison. They reviewed Jim's record and decided (not without reservations) that his recent behavior changes warranted a transfer to Rockview. The day he had been dreaming of, and working for, had finally come.

CHAPTER 5

Rockview

The prison van in which Jim and the others were traveling was cleared to leave Western Penitentiary. It pulled through the gates that thirteen years earlier had opened to Jim and swallowed him up. The van wound slowly through the streets that surrounded the prison, streets that were still flanked by industrial buildings and warehouses, all of which were located on the Ohio River just several miles south of Pittsburgh's downtown Golden Triangle.

Jim was leaving a place of stifling confinement, noise, and grayness. He was headed for central Pennsylvania, a beautiful example of rural America with fertile, wide, green valleys of farmland by the forest-covered mountains of the Appalachian range. As the prison van moved along, wild flowers lined the edges of the country roads, and barns with their silos dotted the countryside. The wide valley gave a sense of space not seen or experienced by Jim in a long time. It was the summer of 1961. It was a beautiful, clear day. By this time he had traveled through the town of State College and was continuing to head east, back into the country. The road was straight for a distance and soon was joined by railroad tracks running parallel to it. All of a sudden a sign appeared that read, "Rockview State Correctional Institution, Bellefonte, PA." On the left there were wide, well-cut lawns sloping up from the road to a beautifully landscaped hillside leading to a large white building that dominated the view of the rest of the valley. This enormous building reminded Jim of pictures he had seen of the white government buildings in Washington, DC. This one, however, did not have pillars in front.

As the van got closer to the building, tall barbed-wire fencing could be seen marking off the prison grounds behind the big building but still attached to it. Smaller brick buildings a couple of stories high were grouped within the barbed-wire fencing. Adding to the impressiveness of the structure was a large formal garden surrounded by a beautiful, waist-high, stone, openwork fence with a stone staircase leading to the lawns in front of the building. From the main road the van turned into a driveway that went past the front entrance to the side where there was a gate in the high fence. The prisoners looked out the window of the van at the fence that stretched as far as the eye could see.

As the van pulled through the gate, instead of seeing an impenetrable fortress before him, Jim saw five or six two-story brick buildings that, he discovered later, contained cell-blocks with about two hundred and fifty cells each. Then visible were other administrative and farm buildings that were landscaped and softened with carefully chosen trees and shrubs.

Eventually escorted to his cell, Jim entered a space of about seven by nine feet with an eight-foot ceiling. The standard urinal, toilet, bunk, and sink were present plus a desk. The ceiling was white, the walls green. From his window he could see the lush green that covered the valley and mountains. The window had a view of the main road on which he had driven to the prison. In addition to the farmland, he was able to see the prison work trucks coming and going, which intensified his drive to get that truck job and escape. How many times a day did he see himself behind the wheel of one of those trucks, pulling through the prison gates onto the main road, never to be seen again.

Though Jim had experienced some significant changes in his life while at Western, such as an increased hunger to read and learn, and an ability to control his violent behavior, the desire for the truck job only intensified, and the violence in his life came out in different ways. What was carried from Western to Rockview was his absolute hatred of the prison guards or anyone in an authority position in the prison. From the standpoint of any prisoner, there were two kinds of people: the inmates and guards, or "us and them." The belief was that no guard ever cared at all about the prisoners. The guards were the enemy. In Western the guards were hated, and there were those inmates who made it their intent each day to make it as difficult for them as they possibly could.

Out of Jim's hatred for guards in general came a hatred for one guard in particular who was generally on night duty. After lights were out would come the sound of footsteps, then silence for a minute, then the slight tapping on the bars of the cell with a billy club, then the footsteps on to the next cell. After a while, it became clear that the guard stood in silence in front of Jim's cell longer than the time he spent in front of any other before continuing his patrol. There welled up in Jim the wish that the guard would be killed. Because Jim wanted to get out of prison so badly, it was clear to him that he wouldn't do the killing. But he spent time each day (mainly after lights-out at night) thinking of ways it could happen. Possibly he could get someone else to do it, but he generally fantasized an accident such as the guardrail along the range collapsing and the terrified guard plummeting to his death a couple of stories below. This was a daily wish, unashamedly savored. *I want you dead, man,* was his constant thought. Two things were certain every night: dealing with his feelings concerning this guard, and reliving Alice's murder through the eventual nightmare of terror.

Daytime was more positive. Once in the population he was put to work immediately and over the summer was involved in a series of work experiences that acquainted him with different aspects of life at Rockview. He was first assigned to a work gang whose job was putting in a new cesspool. It involved going under guard to the nearby mountain to get rocks. This kind of work immediately made Jim aware of his poor physical condition. In Western he did a lot of sitting, but here he needed physical strength. He needed to build strong muscles. With exercise he started feeling better and one reason was that his bowels were moving regularly. Perspiring from hard work also made him feel sharper physically and mentally. He became careful about what he ate and was sleeping better, though the nightmares never ceased. In prison, exercise is up to the individual and he finally realized it.

Jim's prison gang began to work as a team. Faced with getting the rocks from the top of the mountain to the bottom to build the cesspool, they pooled their ideas and ended up digging a notch down the side of a particular slope. The stones could then be rolled down the notch to the exact place where they would be loaded on the truck. Jim thought, *Bein' part of a team like this is sure different than bein' alone and lookin' over your shoulder all the time.* Working hard made the time go by quickly, and many times he would work through his break time. At the end of the day he was tired, with a tiredness that, after a bath, made him relax.

Mr. Mays, his work supervisor, paid close attention to what he was doing and stated, "Jim, you are one of the best workers I've ever had, and I like the way you keep asking questions and showing interest." Jim didn't care whether or not Mr. Mays answered the questions. It was all part of the con of getting a good report.

One of the many projects at the prison was putting in a new water system for the cannery. All the vegetables grown at Rockview were canned on the prison grounds. When one of the prisoners on the project became sick, Jim was put in his place. Because it was somewhat of an emergency, Jim worked nights as well as days. One afternoon the sunshine poured through the windows onto the bins where the vegetables were being sprayed by what Jim described as upside-down showerheads. As fountains of water washed over the beautiful green peas, yellow corn, and red tomatoes, he couldn't remember the last time he had seen anything quite as beautiful as the water intensifying all the different colors. The next day, as he was finishing his work there, he saw a radio on the shelf. He turned it on and the music of Debussy's *La Mer,* one of his favorites, filled the room of the cannery. As he listened and watched the fountains washing the vegetables, he forgot where he was. *This is gorgeous,* he thought.

In another job he helped to refurbish a building. One day he had to fix a windowsill. He installed the frame and Mr. Mays, who called Jim "Joe" because he had another Jim in the work gang, observed the work and said, "Not bad, Joe." Jim, who knew little about concrete, filled in the frame with the mortar he had mixed. A few days later Mr. Mays said, "OK, pull that frame off of there." When the frame was pulled off, the whole sill crumbled and fell to the ground. Mr. Mays then said, "Now I'll tell you what you did wrong." After his explanation Jim said, "Why didn't you tell me this before?" "Then you wouldn't have learned anything," Mr. Mays replied. *Pretty shrewd,* Jim thought.

Working in the fields on the farm was also part of life at Rockview. One day he was picking tomatoes, with a guard giving specific instructions on how the prisoners should mark their baskets. Jim had picked enough tomatoes and other vegetables to fill some thirty baskets. Another prisoner came over to the guard and claimed that he had picked the contents of all the baskets. "No," said the guard. "See the mark? These are all Jim's baskets." The other prisoner came up to Jim and said, "Startin' tomorrow you're gonna put my mark on all your baskets." Jim hadn't fought in a while, but he was ready to at that moment. He responded, "Oh, really? That means that both of us are gonna get locked up startin' tomorrow. You mess with me and that's the end of that!"

Jim had stopped smoking so during break time he sometimes kept working, which occasionally resulted in problems. He had to explain to a supervisor one day, "When I was sittin' during a break, I'd be doin' somethin', like I'd pick up a tool and start cleanin' it. The other day this guard says, 'You're going to clean all the tools and when you get them all done, you're still going out and do your picking and make your quota.' At first I did it, but then I couldn't make the quota. So he wrote me up and I tried to explain and the guard says, 'This is prison'—like I should have been able to do it. Nobody could have done it. So I told him to lock me up, and the guard said, 'What do you mean?' and I said, 'I'm not workin' any more,' and I went and sat down. 'If you think you're gonna have me doin' tools and get my quota too, you're crazy. That's that.'"

The superior listened. He said, "You've got more guts than you have common sense, but this time it's in your favor."

One day a deputy told Jim, "I like you, so I'm gonna let you go out and pick potatoes tomorrow." Jim said, "Well, it's about time you're givin' me a job that don't have too much labor in it." It was then that he found out that in an acre of ground you get several hundred bushels of potatoes. Jim told him later, "Good thing I didn't have a gun! I'm just findin' out you got twenty-five acres of potatoes out there."

When Jim was working in the soil (as far back as Ellwood), he would get caught up in the beauty or profoundness of something in nature. In digging up a potato, he all of a sudden held it, looked at it with all of its eyes, and thought, *Only a little spud or one of them eyes makes this potato. I never thought about this stuff before—how many eyes would it take to plant these twenty-five acres? Huh, new life comes out of the eye.*

Working in the fields and in other projects continued and in the midst of the drudgery at times there was some humor. Purdue was also at Rockview. He had come before Jim, but they got together soon after Jim's arrival. Purdue was a great source of laughs. One day the machine that fed the big furnace broke, and Jim and Purdue were sent to the furnace room to throw the coal into the furnace by the shovelful. They worked strenuously together. When they had finished, Jim was sweating and covered with coal dust and Purdue said, "Boy, you look like my brother now, for sure."

At the time, Rockview was segregated in the dining room and the food line. When prisoners lined up to go to the dining room, the whites were in the front of the line and the blacks were in the back. In the dining room they had their own tables. One day Jim and Purdue came up from the furnace room to the dining room. Jim went and sat with the black men and Purdue sat with the whites. The guard saw this and was embarrassed to challenge the situation. He came up to Purdue and Purdue said, "I ain't sittin' with them." Then the lieutenant came in and said, "Alright, you two, sit over there and sit there from now on." He said to the guard, "Don't pay any attention to them clowns from now on—just write 'em up." It wasn't too long after that that they stopped all segregation in the dining room. Segregation had made no sense to Jim, who had lived with all kinds of people since he went to reform school at the age of eight.

After several months the first interview took place to assess what was going on in Jim's life as well as to present the prison's observations of him. "You know, Jim," the interviewer said, "there are a couple of things that bother me. You have an excellent work report. Your block report is one of the best I've ever seen. As a matter of fact, I don't get it. According to what they told me at Western, you used to fight upon any provocation and even without provocation. You don't seem to do that any more. You've all but stopped cursing. You go to church, but you don't go to school. How come?"

After a moment of thoughtful silence, Jim said, "I read a lot." "Like what?" the interviewer asked. Jim responded, "I like fiction and history and stories about people. Some of my favorite readin' is from *The Reader's Digest*. They call it 'The Most Unforgettable Character.' I also read about Tchaikovsky and I read about Beethoven. Those guys wrote all that music I love, but, boy, they had one horrible life with the stuff they had to deal with. Some things are way over my head like T. S. Elliott, but I'm able to pick up some stuff in it I understand here and there. I read for enjoyment and for what I can learn, like I'd think, 'Oh, is that what that means—huh!'"

Jim said to the interviewer, who was also the librarian at Rockview, "Man, I'm too old to go to school and I'm tired." The interviewer responded, "Oh, we have that all solved." He explained how it would work. In addition to instruction Jim would be allowed to take four tests a year at a cost of one dollar a test. A passing grade provided a credit

point. "And, Jim, you can do this all at your own speed."
Jim's initial thought was, *Forget it.* Then, *But wait, he'll put
it on my record.* He signed up.

Jim passed his algebra test, and as he's often said, "I
couldn't even spell algebra." Many of the questions on the
tests were multiple choice. He'd look at the question and
then look at the answers, and based upon what he could
remember from his studying, he thought, *well, that looks
like the answer.* The area of greatest difficulty was spelling.
He told the instructor, "I can't spell worth a hoot and ya
knew they had questions there askin' which one is right or
which one is wrong. This is tough." He failed the first test
and then the next test would come along. *Well, that answer
didn't work before, let's try another.* One day he passed the
spelling final and, having passed the tests in his other subjects, he ended up with more credits than he needed to get
his G.E.D.

Jim went back to the librarian and asked if there was a
course in history. He didn't know that the librarian was a
history scholar, and he began to supply Jim with book lists
and frequent conversation, which led to his writing papers
every few months. Reading and studying had become essential to his daily life. Another aspect of daily life that eventually became essential for Jim was his involvement in the
chapel program. One day, a fellow inmate who was the janitor in the chapel and chaplain's offices told Jim, "I'm
movin' on. You should take my place." Jim, remembering
his work in the chaplain's office in Western, said, "Come on,
man. That's no place for me." The janitor said, "I've already
talked it over with Father Walsh and he's talked it over with
Mr. Rheems, your boss. Mr. Rheems said he'll miss you, but
agreed that you oughta go up there, given this thing you're
getting involved in."

This "thing" was called The Third Order and it came about this way. When Jim entered Rockview a year and a half earlier, he had been listed as a Catholic so he had to have a mandatory interview with the prison chaplain, Father Richard Walsh. Father Walsh asked, "Are you interested in going to church?" Jim emphatically responded, "Not really." Father Walsh said, "OK" *Why doesn't he get mad or say you oughta go?* Jim thought. After about a month Father Walsh came to Jim and said, "You know, we are starting a Third Order of Saint Francis, an order for lay people." Jim asked, "Who's Saint Francis and what's a Third Order? Why don't you just shove it, Father!" Father Walsh said, "Alright," and left. But then Jim thought, *Jim, you should do this. It will be on your record. Remember the truck job!* He went to the chaplain's office and asked, "What do you do in all this Third Order stuff?" Father Walsh had a schedule which required that they all meet together to study scripture, go to Mass, go to confession, and receive communion. "Jim, why don't you give it a try?"

At the first meeting, Father Walsh talked about Saint Francis and his example, and how each of the prisoners could take his life and use it for good. Father told the gathering, "Start to look at this prison like a monastery—you get up early in the morning, have a regular schedule of prayer, work, meals, and so on." He introduced the idea of making sacrifices. Possibly they would give up a dessert or something important to them because it is a way of saying "thanks" to the Lord for all that he had done for them. Then he told everyone that meetings would take place every Friday. Jim thought, *This is a bunch of bull, but I'll go anyway.* At the end of the meeting Jim went to the priest and said, "You know, I shot my mouth off at the meeting, but I think I will do what you said about confession and communion." Father Walsh said, "That's great!" He wasn't fooled, however. He knew a con artist when he saw one.

Every first Saturday Jim went to confession and would make up some outrageous story of sexual impurity. Father Walsh, with great compassion, said he understood because it takes time to get used to being celibate. Then he told him to say three "Our Fathers" for his penance. *I'm not botherin' with all this penance bull,* Jim thought, *but I will keep doin' these meetings and confession.*

It had been a year and a half since Jim's first involvement with the Third Order, which is one reason why the janitor and Mr. Rheems recommended him to be the new janitor in the chaplain's office. Janitorial duties started immediately and, as was the case at Western Penitentiary, Jim soon found himself getting involved with his fellow prisoners who came to the chaplain's office for help. In conversations he would inevitably end up making three suggestions: "Go to school, read the newspaper, and go to church."

One inmate, in conversation with Jim, said, "Why should I read the newspaper?" Jim said, "Listen, when you come to a place like this, a couple of years later what used to be don't exist any more. Cars will be different, prices different, and if you keep up with them, you'll have an idea of what things are about. When you get outta here, you won't suddenly be smacked in the face." This kind of involvement with the inmates was reported back: "Jim in the chaplain's office said I oughta do this or that and I'm glad I did what he said."

As his involvement in the Third Order continued, studying its reading materials took more of Jim's attention. *I really need to know what I'm getting' into* was a recurring thought. *What do I really have to do before makin' my first profession, if I make one?* He kept studying and Father

Walsh was faithful in always giving him affirmation and encouragement concerning the good job he was doing, the moment it was merited. One day, however, Jim did something he never did again. He was wondering, *What's it really that Father writes about me on my record? My report's comin' up soon.* Jim picked the lock of the file drawer, pulled out his file and read it, and then put it back immediately. He stood before the file cabinet, not being able to move. He was mortified that he had done it and momentarily paralyzed with shame. *O Lord God, I am so sorry,* his insides moaned. *But then, are all these great things he's sayin' about me really true? I have to sit down. My legs are shakin'—they are nothin' under me. Nobody ever said stuff like this about me—ever. Father is really my brother and father. Oh, why did I do this? How can I look Father in the eye?* He couldn't. It took days before he could even look at him again.

As the Third Order meetings continued, the more Jim realized he wanted to please Father Walsh and wanted his acceptance. The more Jim was with him, the more he watched him and how he operated with the other inmates. *Do you deal with the other guys like you deal with me? Do you walk your talk? Are you real?* These questions were answered immediately as he overheard a conversation between Father Walsh and an inmate who was in the hole. Father Walsh said to the inmate, "How are you doing?" The inmate said, "What the f-ck do you care?" Father Walsh responded with, "Not a f-cking thing, just checking to see if you're OK." Jim thought, *This kind of language never bothers him and he never judges anyone. He does walk his talk, but I don't. I feel bad. I keep givin' him a con job, tellin' him what he wants to hear most of the time.*

CHAPTER 6

Thomas Merton

As Father Walsh handed the thick book across his desk, Jim wondered how long it would take him to read it. When Jim took it, their eyes met, and Father Walsh stated, "I really hope you'll read this, Jim, and see if you connect with Merton in any way." The book was *Seven Storey Mountain* by Thomas Merton. Merton had become a well-known Catholic priest and his book was receiving considerable attention at the time. Jim had never heard of Merton or his writing.

After work that evening Jim opened the book and soon discovered that it was unlike any reading he had ever done in the past. This was not a Zane Grey novel. He realized he had to read it slowly and reread those parts in which he felt a connection between himself and Merton. Through the following days he also came to the realization that he could not read it without having someone to talk with about it. Some of the Third Order members asked him one day what the book was about. Jim told them, "It's the story of this guy who was really brilliant. In his twenties he was searching, tryin' all kinds of stuff—a lot not good—to find meaning and to stop his rottenness. It was through all of his readin', and some special people in his life, that he began to become interested in all this spiritual hocus pocus and then God." Jim went on to say, "Our actual stories are different, but as far as I've gotten in the book, there are some things we went through that are similar. Thus far I'm somehow connectin' with where he's goin'. He keeps makin' me think about stuff from the past like, one of the first things that grabbed me was his talkin' about his father. Unlike me, Merton had a good time with his dad. His dad had a different way of dealin' with things. For example, Merton says...." and Jim read to them the following passage:

> The only really valuable religious and moral training I ever got as a child came to me from my father, not systematically, but here and there and more or less spontaneously in the course of ordinary conversations. Father never applied himself, or set purpose to teach me religion, but if something spiritual was on his mind it came out more or less naturally.*

Jim went on, "That statement takes me back to rememberin' my dad. I always had to go to church. There were times he'd have no chance to clean up after work, but we went to church anyway. I was thinkin' back that things I know today I know 'cause we always went to church. We didn't have a father-son relationship—we fell out—but I'm beginnin' to realize at this stage how glad I am that he dragged me. Maybe it was gettin' me ready for where I am now.

"You know, guys, Merton really stopped me again as I was readin' the other day. He was talkin' about bein' brought to see deep parts of his insides, like when he was in his room one night and his light was on and he felt like his father, who had died a year earlier, was there in the same room. Imagin'! Ya know, he loved his father and admired him and thought he was a great guy. But with all this stuff goin' on, he got a look at himself and that sure wasn't how he saw his old man." Again, Jim read:

---

*Thomas Merton, *The Seven Storey Mountain* (San Diego/New York: Harcourt Brace & Company, 1948), 53.

Instantly I was overwhelmed with a sudden and profound insight into the misery and corruption of my own soul. I was filled with horror with what I saw, and my whole being rose up in revolt against what was within me, and my soul desired escape liberation and freedom from all of this.... (p. 111)

"I groan and hurt this way inside too," Jim said. "I feel all his words. I'm not seein' special things so much as just feelin' the pain. I know there's somethin' here for me that's gonna show me who I am, but do I have to become filled with more fear and terror than I already have in nightmares? It never stops."

The next day Jim read where Merton quotes 2 Peter 3: "The Lord dealeth patiently for your sake, not willing that any should perish, but that all should return to penance" (p. 129).

If this isn't bull, Jim thought, *then for me it's too good to be true. Does this include me, Jimmy Townsend—so that I wouldn't perish?* In talking to Father Walsh about this, Father said, "The promise is that Jesus is 'not willing that any should perish.'"

"Yeah, Father," Jim replied. "I remember hearin' in one of our meetins one day about Jesus standin' at the door knockin', and there is no door knob on his side 'cause he will not force his way in. You have to open that door. If I opened that door, would Jesus be there for me? If you remember me tellin' you, people bein' there for me in the past was nothin' I experienced much. It's tough tryin' to believe this promise. *Is it a promise or bull?*

"Ya know, Father," Jim continued, "Merton in his searchin' got around to a lot of places and into a lot of experiences in Europe and America and other parts of the world. He was tryin' to get it together. In one part of his travels he talked about his time spent at Columbia University in New York and his gettin' connected to the Communist party there and dealin' with Communist doctrine and promises. After bein' a part of it for awhile, he is sayin' that it is dumb for them Communists, who are members of the human race like us, who in followin' Communist beliefs have changed only their minds. They changed their ideology to the Communist belief, but it didn't move out of their minds to really help people. People suffered. He's sayin', who do they think they are that they 'should suddenly turn around and produce a perfect society when they have never been able in the past to produce anything but imperfection and, at best, the barest shadow of justice' (p. 135).

"Father, I read this and began imaginin' and thinkin' what Merton had been thinkin' before he came to these thoughts. He probably was thinkin', 'Communism is really neat. It's gonna solve a lot of problems. Everybody's gonna be treated alike.' But knowin' how his story ends up, I was wonderin' if this Lord he was searchin' for was sayin' to him, 'You better think about this Communist stuff again, man.'

"As I read his comment about Communism, I think it was startin' to come together for him that only the card-carrying Communists were the ones who had the food. Lots of people were starvin' to death under Stalin so all that stuff of 'everything for the state' was a bunch of bull. It wasn't for everybody. I'm soundin' like I'm runnin' off here. What I'm tryin' to say, and what's important to me here, is that I'm realizin' that stuff in Merton's life wasn't altogether at that time, and I was thinkin', 'I don't have it together, either.' Merton was gettin' some answers. And lookin' back and seein' where I am now, I certainly got some answers, but I just don't understand them all. I do know that over a period of time some things have started to get clear. I guess I have to trust that somehow it will come together for me as it did for Merton. This is really tough readin' for me."

Father responded, "Don't stop reading, Jim."

At a meeting the following week, part of the Third Order discussion centered around the sinful things they had done that they couldn't seem to control. Jim said, "I was just readin' some things about this in Merton. Ya know, Merton led a wild life. We sure have had that same experience. Let me read you what I read last night. He was sayin' he didn't know what would have happened to him 'if my nature had been more stubborn in clinging to the pleasures that disgusted me, if I had refused to admit that I was beaten by this futile search for satisfaction where it could not be found' (p. 164).

"I remember tellin' you about them sex nights in the woods in Pittsburgh with Big Dad and Mom and Judy and all that gang and how I wanted that all the time, but how it all humiliated me and how awful I felt. But where Merton here kinda gave up because he couldn't find the satisfaction he was lookin' for, I was kinda taken away from it because of Alice. She opened me up to somethin' I never knew or experienced before and somethin' I didn't fully understand, yeah, and something I didn't really know what to do with. *Oh, the nightmares.*" Jim went on, "Now listen to this part: 'I had to come very far to find myself in this blind alley, but the very anguish and helplessness of my position was something to which I rapidly succumbed. And it was my defeat that was to be the occasion of my rescue' (p. 165).

"Guys," Jim said, "I want to tell you that my defeat, I'm beginnin' to realize, was in the stupidity of my life. I was lookin' back over everything and I'm realizin', 'I shoulda done this and not that, or vice versa.' One day in my cell I began thinkin' about the commandments in scripture we was talkin' about in a meetin' the other day. There was this guy who came up to Jesus and asked, 'Hey! What's the greatest commandment?' Jesus answered, 'You're to love the Lord your God with all your heart, soul, mind, and thoughts.' But then the Lord said, 'The other one is just as great: Love your neighbor as yourself. And in these two all the things rest.' This is it!

"It kinda hit me, 'Well, if you do them two, you can't fail to do all the other ones. They're right there in the box, in the frame, however ya put it.' Is this the way to my rescue—love your neighbor as yourself? How do I love someone else, when I don't love myself? All this stuff came together. Good grief! If I'd have just kept my mouth shut when I shoulda kept it shut, or kept my hands to myself, or just went ahead and done my work. Stupid! In seein' my defeat, am I now bein' rescued?"

Outside of his work detail, Jim spent a lot of time alone reading and reflecting. He couldn't remember anywhere in scripture where Jesus asked whether a person had the right talents or if they were educated or how much they had achieved or how nice they were. *He just asks me to be with him,* he thought. *Yeah, like God told Moses to go rescue Israel, and Moses said 'I can't talk too good.' Then God told him to go and he'd tell him what to say. Huh, maybe even you, Jimmy, could be rescued, and there could be somethin' for you to do just like you are.*

The time Jim most looked forward to was after work when he could read. One night he looked up from the Merton book and thought, *What is he talkin' about anyway? How many more times do I have to read this?* He read it again: "Indeed, outside of Him there is nothing, and whatever exists exists by His free gift of its being" (p. 169).

With the book under his arm, Jim went to the next Third Order meeting and read this same passage to them.

Then he said, "What's stoppin' me now in Merton is the 'Outside of Him there is nothing' statement. I don't know about that. I don't believe it yet, but I know that somethin' is happenin' to me and I don't understand it."

For a couple of seconds Jim's mind digressed to an experience he'd had the night before, when he had first read that quote. He had thought about getting the truck job. But where previously it had occupied almost every waking moment, last night he realized that he hadn't thought about it in days, a week possibly! Leaving his thoughts, he then said to the group, "All I know is that I'm in a better place in my gut and I'm not doin' the changin'. I don't know how this happened."

"Jim," said one of the group members, "can I tell you where I've felt another change is taking place in you?" Jim nodded consent. "I could be wrong, but I've been hearing less and less about your bad attitude toward the Church and, as you say, 'all their hocus-pocus bull.' There's something different here."

Some group members leaned forward in their chairs waiting to hear Jim's answer. It took a few minutes. He was looking down at his hands folded in his lap. Finally he looked up at everyone and said, "I don't know why I didn't say somethin' today or last week. I guess I'm tryin' to figure out what's happenin' and it's not all that clear. Let me read to you what I read last week from Merton that I think says somethin' about what you're askin'." Jim then explained that in his search, Merton said he had

acquired an immense respect for Catholic philosophy and for the Catholic faith. Further than that it seemed I could not go, for the time being....How many there are in the same situation! In a certain sense, these people have a better appreciation of the Church and of Catholicism than many Catholics, an appreciation which is detached and intellectual and objective. But they never come to the Church. They stand and stare in the doors of the banquet—the banquet to which they surely realize that they are invited—while those more poor, more stupid, less gifted, less educated, sometimes even less virtuous than they, enter in and are filled at those tremendous tables. (p. 175)

Jim went on talking about Merton with all of his arguments and problems with the Church and then read aloud the following:

When I stopped thinking explicitly about all of its arguments, its effect began to show itself in my life. I began to have a desire to go to church and a desire more sincere and mature and deep seated than I had ever had before. After all, I had never before had so great a need. (p. 175)

"I believe I'm feelin' some of this same stuff," Jim said. "Like in my job. My assignment is to maintain the chapel. I know that when I go to work in the chapel, if I do a good job and the floor shines *and* the pews shine, then they say, 'Well, he's a good worker. He learns fast.' Like Merton havin' a growin' desire to get to church, I have a growin' desire to be here to do my job. This is my job, my territory. I'm thinkin' that I'm not tryin' to blow my own horn—'I did this—look at what I did over here.' What's more important to me is that I gave a nice clean place to the guys who come in and sit down and maybe get somethin'. In fact, every once in awhile someone would say, 'Boy, you sure do make a floor shine.'

"I remember one day a guy came in and said, 'What's your trick on the floor?' And he passed out when I told him, 'I don't use as much wax as your guys use. I won't put more wax on this year.' I told him it was a matter of sweepin' it once a week and usin' a cold-water mop on it once a week, and then buffin' it on Saturday before all the services started, and doin' the same thing on Monday to knock out what was messed up. Ya know, I guess when I get down to it, the thoughts about the job bein' my job—my territory—are now less important than really wantin' to please someone." *But, Jimmy,* he said to himself, *don't forget they may not be as frequent, but you still got those thoughts about that truck job and gettin' out of here!*

"I think about Merton's need to be in church," he said to the group. "My need at first to be in church concerned doin' my job to get me away from the other stuff goin' on in prison and to keep me away from the demons, from the nightmares. But, you know, like I said, gradually other things are startin' to be important—like I find myself sayin' the Rosary while I am workin' in the chapel. Or, in my own way, as I'm moppin' or buffin', I do all the Stations of the Cross and say an 'Our Father.'" He thought again, *Is this really becomin' more important to me than gettin' the truck job to escape?*

One afternoon in the chaplain's office, Father Walsh asked him, "How's the book going?"

"Father," Jim responded, "as I go along readin' about this guy—he is smart—it's hard for me to believe our lives have a lot of the same stuff. It really grabs me."

Getting a copy of the book from his desk, Father Walsh said, "Let me read you this: '[A]nd so it was with me. Books and ideas and poems and stories, pictures and music, build-ings, cities, places, philosophies were to be the materials upon which grace would work' (p. 178). Now what do you think of that?'"

Jim answered, "I know I don't like poems 'cause I really can't read a poem and get stuff out of it. But I can listen to someone else read a poem and get stuff out of it. After readin', I'd look at the poem and say to the guy, 'How'd you get all that out of it, huh?' Now books and movin' pictures and classical music I love. With the music I can't pronounce all the words but I can sit back and be as contented as can be. A lot of times I'd be sittin' in my house [cell] listenin' to somethin'—the next thing I knew I'd be sayin' a 'Hail Mary' and the 'Our Father.' Or I'd be thinkin' of someone and I'd pray, 'Lord, give him or her a touch of this or that.' These kinds of things Merton was talkin' about take me into prayer with what little I know about it, and the music especially takes me into my feelings.

"Father, you just read that poem and music and stuff—where is it on the page—here—'were to be the materials upon which grace would work.' So maybe grace is workin' in me. I read a couple a days ago what Merton says about grace. Let me find it here. Yeah, here it is. 'What is grace? It is God's own life shared by us. God's life is love' (p. 169). So, Father, God is workin' in me through these things I love, like the music."

Father responded with a smile and said, "That is why you needed to hear this quote."

That night in his cell, Jim was reading further and he was challenged regarding the significance of his group, the Third Order: "...that God brought me and a half a dozen others together at Columbia and made us friends in such a way that our friendship would work powerfully to rescue us from the confusion and misery in which we had come to find ourselves" (p. 178).

Jim thought, *Yeah, I too know it inside myself that I have been brought together with a bunch of others at my "Columbia"—this prison. We've become friends and connected as we are part of the Third Order Franciscans and I think Father and the guys trust me. Things are better for me 'cause we have been brought together. Ya know, Mr. Merton, one of the things that keeps grabbin' me about you is that you're not comin' up with a lot of fast answers. You were in a long struggle like me. I'm halfway through readin' your book and you're still fightin' stuff. It's like the time you made a trip to Olean, New York, the home of one of your friends. While there, your friend wanted to see a former friend of his who was the librarian at Saint Bonaventure, a college run by the Franciscans. His friend liked the library and wanted to show it and the campus to you. But you refused to get out of the car to go see the library. Then you wrote*

Let's get going. I don't know what was the matter. Perhaps I was scared of the thought of nuns and priests being all around me—the elemental fear of the citizens of hell, in the presence of anything that savors the religious life, religious vows, official dedication to God through Christ Too many crosses. Too many holy statues. Too much quiet and cheerfulness. Too much pious optimism. It made me very uncomfortable. I had to flee. (p. 201)

Man, I really hear that! Jim thought. *You shoved my past in my face. I hated priests and nuns 'cause I thought they were a bunch of jerks. Priests were goin' around and sayin' this and that in all of this Latin bull. You never knew exactly what they were sayin' while they were wavin' their hands around and all that. The nuns were those crazy women with all those clothes on. They didn't go out or do nothin'. Yeah, I understand what you were sayin', Mr. Merton, but I'm realizin' at this point that I'm seein' things different. Maybe it is because of Father Walsh and the Third Order.*

The next morning Jim's train of thought continued. *How I'm thinkin' right now is that the priest in a sense is like a father, which I guess is why they call him Father. He's not takin' the Lord's place, but he's workin' in conjunction with the Lord as His right-hand man.* His thoughts then went to the nuns. *The nuns are like a wife in a sense. They take care of the kids in school and they're like nurses and teachers. But they don't have to leave their work to go home and take care of their family. They can stay 'till the job is done. Huh, these are new thoughts.*

It seemed to be taking Jim a long time getting through *Seven Storey Mountain,* as he would spend a lot of time either savoring some of Merton's thoughts, identifying with him, or just rereading particular chapters, trying to understand what he was saying. He brought passage after passage to Father Walsh for clarification and understanding. At this point he was now leading some Third Order meetings, and content from Merton was more frequently presented and discussed by the group. This helped Jim sort through a level of thinking that was not easy and also discover that changes were taking place in his inner self.

He was particularly arrested by Merton's book one day and brought the paragraph to the group for reflection and discussion:

Whoever you are, the land to which God has brought you is not like the land of Egypt from which you came out. You can no longer live here as you lived there.

Your old life and former days are crucified now, and you must not seek to live anymore for your gratification, but give up your own judgment into the hands of a wise director, and sacrifice your pleasures and comforts for the love of God, and give the money to the poor. (p. 232)

After several moments of silence Jim said, "I realized in readin' this where I really am in my heart. I'm no longer in Egypt. When I am in the chapel, I am home. I am in his home, which doesn't have a lot of frills in it, and yet that is the most important time in my day. I dust, I mop, I buff, I pray. I might have gotten up feelin' tired, but then I wasn't tired anymore. When I go to my house [cell], I lay down and go to sleep. A lot of times I lay there and start thinkin' about things that happened during the day. I'd be there on my bunk and think of somethin' and then I'd work up a speech and imagine sixty people in front of me and I'd give a speech on the subject. If I do say so myself, some amazin' things pop into my head.

"Like the other day, I was made aware of an exciting possibility. Merton said, 'God calls men—not only religious, but all kinds of Christians—to be the salt of the earth' (p. 291). I got to thinkin' that he's gonna let me be salt, and salt, how should I say it, lifts up the flavors. Then I thought that you could overdo salt. Too much of it makes stuff sour or bitter. Father Walsh says, 'To have it just right is to be just you.' I'm tryin' to learn to accept that. From what I'm seein' thus far, I'm being used to do stuff with the chaplain and the Third Order just as I am. I don't have to be someone special. I'm not puttin' on airs and stuff. Father Walsh says if you come to somethin' and say, 'Oh, no, I can't do this' all you gotta do is say, 'Lord, by myself I can't do this.' I guess I'm not in Egypt any more.

"Guys, I guess I'm beginnin' to see I can be salt just as an ordinary person. Merton wasn't sayin' this to somebody who's the most famous or most powerful. But what I'm gettin' from this is that the Lord needs someone as he is who's gonna be willin' to be with and where the action is. I want to do this, but to be able to be salt, I realize, is not possible without this 'grace' I'm learnin' about. Merton is showin' us how to get it:

> 'I did not have lofty theories about the vocation of a lay contemplative. In fact, I no longer dignified what I was trying to do by the name of a vocation. All I knew was that I wanted grace and that I needed prayer, and that I was helpless without God, and that I wanted to do everything that people did to keep close to Him.' (p. 301)

"Guys," Jim continued, "this is how the grace is there to do the stuff he wants us to do to 'keep close to Him.' I'm not hearin' anything that says you have to be good to get grace. I hope not, 'cause I got a lot of bad thoughts. Like Merton I'm realizin' more and more feelins of bein' helpless in tryin' to stop em, like I'd wake up sayin' to myself, 'What about this, what about that?' Guys, I'm feelin' that where I am right now is where Merton was and what I want is whatever...'people did to keep close to Him.' I'm feelin' like there's stuff that isn't important to me anymore. I'm baffled. How did I get here? The simpler my life is becomin', the more filled I'm gettin'. You could go to the store and buy a $500 pair of shoes just to show off, but it wouldn't do a thing for your feet! What I'm doin' now in the Third Order is more important than anything I've ever known."

That night, after the meeting and before lights-out, Jim read:

> I belonged to God, not to myself: and to belong to Him is to be free, free of all anxieties and worries and sorrows that belong to the earth and the love of the things that are in it. What was the difference between one place and another, one habit and another, if your life belonged to God, and if you placed yourself completely in His hands? The only thing that mattered was the fact of the sacrifice, the essential dedication of oneself. The rest was accidental. (p. 370)

Jim thought, *Merton, you finally got your wish. It was the end of your search. Here I am in Rockview readin' all these weeks. Right now where's this peace comin' from? There's a happiness like I've not known before. I feel trusted by Father and the brothers* [his fellow members of the Third Order]. *They keep sayin' good things about me and I have work to do. Am I missin' something in some other place by havin' to be here? Ha! I don't know any other place. I haven't been to any other place in so long I forgot what "out there" looks like, but I do know what I have here. I guess I'm not in Egypt any more.*

Then he read Merton's account of finally entering the monastery in Kentucky: "So Brother Matthew locked the gate behind me and I was enclosed in the four walls of my new freedom" (p. 372).

Tears welled up in Jim. Since this was a rare occurrence, he had very little practice in controlling them. He was trying to think of why this statement of Merton so penetrated his thick armor. *When I entered Western with its thick walls, the door slammed shut and I had no freedom. But what's happenin' to me? Here at Rockview I am still behind four walls—no, four fences. I still can't get out, but for the first time in my whole life I have peace and joy and I know love. This is a new place I have never been before. I'm all alone here in this new place. I'm scared. I'm in this place I don't understand and did nothin' to get to. I'm afraid because there's a new power that's taken over. I don't know what to do with it all.*

CHAPTER 7

Mr. Slick

It had taken a lifetime for Jim to build the impenetrable walls that protected him from himself and the violent forces around him. These walls were now not just crumbling, they were falling down. Jim's walls had protected him from attackers and from facing himself and his feelings, but his defense systems didn't know how to combat and stop the onslaught of the gifts of freedom, joy, and love that he now experienced. Feelings and fears that had been stifled for years finally broke through his fortress walls. He fell back on his bunk and convulsed from inner places of remorse and despair that had been buried for so long he didn't know that they had ever existed.

The next day was Saturday, the day he had to go to confession. Exhausted, Jim went and knelt down. *I can't do my phony routine any more,* he thought. *I can't come to confession any more and make up stories. I'm scared.* As Jim knelt in the confessional booth, Father Walsh opened the little door and said, "Can I help you?" Jim said, "Yeah. I need a whole lot of help." Father Walsh said, "Well, Jim, it's about time." *Oh my God, how does he know it is me?* Jim thought. *You're not supposed to know who is confessin'.* Father Walsh told Jim to come to his office when confessions were over.

"How did you know it was me, Father?" Jim asked when he got there.

He answered, "Jim, priests are like mechanics. We know our stock. We know where the problems are. I know your voice. All this time since you've been at Rockview, I've had to give you the rope you needed. If you look back at some of the things I told you, they have all led up to this moment." They talked for the next two hours. They talked about Jim's life from the beginning, his hatreds, his breaking into houses and stealing, and the harm he had done to many people. They talked about how unfair people were to him, especially his father and brother. They talked about his early life, his family, and all the ways he scared and hurt his parents. He was a rapist, and they looked at his victims, his motives for marrying Alice, his cheating, the murder, and on it went. They talked about the ways he had lied to and conned Father Walsh and manipulated people. At the end of two hours there was nothing left in Jim to look at. Jim thought, *Lord, I am totally at your mercy. There are no words left to tell you about my sorrow for what I did or who I became. There is nothin' left in me to deserve your forgiveness or to make me look better to others or myself.*

Father Walsh looked at Jim, completely drained and spent, and said, "Now let's go and make a confession."

Jim said, "What do you think I've been doin' for the last two hours?"

Father said, "Oh, we've been talking as buddies, between you and me. Now let's talk with the Lord." Father put on his stole and Jim made his confession, his first true confession. Father prayed and said, "*Ego te absolvo.* In the name of Jesus Christ, I absolve you from all of your sins. Now go and say three 'Our Fathers.'"

"Father! What did you say? This can't be!" All of a sudden Jim finally saw the scenario of the past year, playing church and playing games with Father Walsh, in all of its reality. He had used the chaplain and the chaplain's office to get a good record for the sake of getting the truck job. Jim remembered coming every Saturday to give Father Walsh what he thought he wanted to hear, with phony, trumped-up confessions. Father then would give him his penance. Jim knew that a penance was to be equal to the sin committed, but he remembered at this moment that all Father Walsh had ever told him to do for penance was to say three "Our Fathers." This basically was no penance at all, and Jim just realized that it reflected the level of his seriousness at the time, which Father saw.

Jim also realized that having just made the confession of his life, coming to the Lord before his priest in absolute brokenness and despair, expecting and wanting to have to pay an enormous price in a penance because he deserved it, Father had merely said again, "Go and say three 'Our Fathers.'" Jim saw again the humbling mercy of God and the extent of his love for him.

Jim later told Father Walsh, "The important thing is that I made a deal with the Lord. As I finished my confession, received forgiveness, and saw God's mercy workin' in me, and then finished my conversation with you, I realized that when two guys make a deal, they shake hands on it. I made a deal in thanksgivin' for his love and what he'd done for me and what he was doin' for me. It wasn't a matter of just two people talkin'—a bond was reached and that was it. The bargain sounded like this to me inside my heart: 'Jim, put yourself in my hands and give your life to me, and I'll lead you and work with you, and I'll know you and you'll know me.'

"You know, Father, at that moment I thought of the thieves on the crosses next to Jesus. Them two guys, both of them were a couple of bums. And they probably didn't know their rear end from a hole in the ground. One guy proved it when he said, 'Come on, man, get us down off this darn thing. If you are Jesus, save yourself and us.' He wasn't interested in the fact that Jesus was an innocent man suffering. But the other guy seen somethin'. Whatever it was, he said, 'Hey, you know we're here because we're supposed to be here, but this guy never did nothin' wrong.' He recognized that. He said, 'Remember me today in Paradise.' And Jesus said, 'You'll be with me there today, man.' That's just what happened. When you stop to think about it, you figure back in them days the average age was probably twenty-five, thirty years, or somethin' like that. He was probably a criminal all his life, and in ten minutes he was in heaven.

"Like the criminal I too made a good confession. I've been forgiven and now Jesus and I are together forever." The tears poured from the center of his being as he sat with his face in his hands. He lost track of time. When he finally regained his composure and knew that there were more fears he hadn't seen yet, there was a long silence and then he said to Father Walsh, "I'm no longer concerned about gettin' out of prison." *The truck job!* he thought. "I am already a free man. I could never experience more freedom than I have right now. I'm no longer the state's prisoner though I'm still in this place. I'm no longer a prisoner of my rage and the angry stuff I did in my first twenty years. Ya know, I'm really God's prisoner."

Sleep that night was elusive. Jim lay in his bunk in the darkness of his cell, reviewing over and over his meeting with Father Walsh and his realization, *I never felt safe like this in my whole life.* The next day Father Walsh said, "When you are ready, I think we need to talk some more about the people in your life." When that time came, several days later, Father directed Jim to think about all the people he had hurt. They were reviewed, one by one. He and Father Walsh prayed that their memories would be healed from all the destructiveness Jim had caused. To review each name was to relive each incident and to see more clearly the resulting devastation. *Oh Lord, I hurt so many people, so many women. I conned and raped, and then—Alice. Lord, where are the words for how sorry I feel?* The convulsive sobbing began again and the muscles in his abdomen began to spasm with pain. It seemed like his body was breaking into thousands of pieces, never to be found again. During the almost daily meetings with Father Walsh, Jim began to realize the difficulty in forgiving himself though he knew that God had forgiven him. Each time Jim and Father came together, he took Jim in prayer before the Lord and asked that he finally would be able to let go of his guilt and self-condemnation, and that his memories would be healed. Father Walsh then gave Jim an exercise to use daily, hourly, or as often as he thought about it. He was to repeat, "I forgive myself and others."

At their next meeting Father began by stating, "Jim, we've talked and prayed about you and about all of those you hurt through the years. I know that this has been very painful for you to go through again, but now I would like us to take a look together at what all your tears are about. I think it would be helpful for your understanding of what's been going on in you. Do you want to think about it and let me know if this is something you're willing to do?"

"No," Jim responded. "I want to do it now! But you gotta understand that I probably can't do this without losin' it. I can't seem to control my emotions." The expression on Father Walsh's face assured Jim of his understanding and compassion. Finally Jim spoke. "Ya know, I just didn't dream up all by myself all of this stuff happenin' to me like bein' forgiven and that. I just feel like someone's spent a long time lookin' for me and finally found me and what tears me up is that I musta been worth lookin' for. O Jesus, I can't believe this."

"Believe it," Father responded.

After several more moments of silence, Jim said, "Then I'm thinkin' how can this be? The other day you had me lookin' at all the people I hurt and destroyed physically or emotionally. Yeah! One by one." Jim struggled for control. "I did terrible things to them. How would there be forgiveness, Father? Why would anybody want me?"

Father responded, "You now know that the Lord Jesus wants you and has for a long time."

Jim nodded and said, "I know it's true he's forgiven me, and while we're talkin' about the pain I caused, I'm right now knowin' and feelin' his love for me. But don't you understand that I can't believe it all could be true. And yet it is. This is where the tears come from. He actually did all this in me and, yeah, for me, and I don't deserve it. This is where the tears come from. This is where the tears come from....Oh, Lord."

The self-hate and rejection did not go away immediately, but one morning, upon awakening, there came from the center of Jim's being an astounding awareness. Because there seemed to be no obstacles in the way of seeing it, no clouds of doubt around it, no moment of self-condemnation to block it, a crystal-clear reality emerged. It welled up as a statement: "Lord, you are real."

Jim was beyond any sense of time and was unaware of how long he lay there, stunned by the reality of this powerful awareness. In the quiet there began to emerge a review and an understanding of the path he had been on all of his life. *Lord, you've been with me all these years in all of this mess, settin' me up to bring me to yourself. What a con artist you are. Yeah! You gave me a chance to listen to and to love classical music to help me get through my messed-up family. You gave me the interest in readin' and wantin' to learn so one day I would be able to read Merton. You gave me the opportunity to come to Rockview so I'd work on my behavior and do do-goody stuff with the chaplain's office so you could drop me next to Father Walsh. You are slick. You knew just how to reach me. You out-conned Jim Townsend, the great con artist. Yeah, now I know you are my Savior and Lord, but I am callin' you Mr. Slick from now on. You are one big operator. I love you. Lord, you are real.*

Jim's mother, Kit Townsend

Detail of Jim Townsend
from below—

Secular Franciscans, Rockview, 1963–64

Jim as a
Franciscan
novice,
Annapolis

Br. Jim Townsend—June 1997

Jim's father, Pat Townsend

A Prisoner of God

CHAPTER 8

Ministry in Prison and Beyond

Jim could have spent the remainder of his life lying in his bunk resting in the unbelievable wonder of what he had experienced, but his duties in the Third Order and in the chaplain's office called him out of his reverie and into activity.

One day a new truckload of prisoners came to Rockview. Part of Jim's job in the chaplain's office was to go to the area where new prisoners were received and give out packets of information on the chapel programs, worship-service schedule, the Third Order, and other activities. Jim had just arrived when the truck pulled up, and he stood watching the prisoners disembark. As he watched, he suddenly heard himself say aloud, "Oh, my God!" A guy in his late teens got off the truck, and as soon as Jim took one look at him, he knew at once that the youth would be eaten alive as soon as he entered the population. Jim thought, *He puts Marilyn Monroe to shame. What a good lookin' guy, blond hair and blue eyes! He is in for trouble. The thought went through his mind: Alice had blond hair and blue eyes. This guy could have been my son.*

The teen's name was Bill. Bill further got Jim's attention when he came up the line to get his packet and said, "Hey, do you by any chance know Jim Townsend?" Jim said, "Well, yeah." Bill said, "Tom So-and-So said for me to see Jim Townsend." Jim said to himself, *What's this clown tryin' to do?* So he said, "When you come over to the chapel for your interview with Father Walsh, I'll introduce you to this Jim Townsend." When Bill came to the chapel, Jim introduced himself, took him into a side room, and said, "If you're tryin' to pull anything, you'll be in trouble right now."

"No, no, I want to talk with you. I'm not as dumb as I look. I know what goes on in prison. This Tom at Western told me you could help me. I'm scared I could be raped."

Jim said, "OK. But if you mess up, there's not a place they can put you where I won't get to you."

"Don't worry," Bill replied. "I'll give you my commissary as payment for your looking after me!" (The commissary was an allowance the prisoners got each month).

"I don't want your commissary," Jim said. At Western he had seen many young men fought over or gang-raped if they didn't have a protector, young men who were beaten and sexually abused because they were at the mercy of those stronger than they were. *There are no privileges in prison, no private quarters except the isolation of the hole. There is no place for Bill to hide, Jim thought. There must be something I can do about this.* He thought a minute and then heard himself say aloud, "I don't care what anyone thinks of this." Jim then made it known to a few key inmates, whom he knew would spread the word, that Bill was "his boy." To the other inmates, this meant that Jim was going to use Bill sexually. It also meant that if anyone else touched Bill, they would have to fight Jim. Everyone knew without question that Jim would back up his promise. He then took Bill under his wing, not as a lover, but as a son. After several weeks Jim reflected, *He is like a son to me. I really care for his well-being.* Jim realized this when Bill reported that he had gotten a C on an exam he had taken in one of his courses. Jim whomped him on the back of the head and said, "You can do better than that." Bill responded, "You sound just like my mother!" Jim thought, *Ha! What he doesn't know is that* I'm *not capable of gettin' a "C" on a test!*

Late one afternoon Jim realized that he hadn't seen Bill all day. He wasn't at meals or in the prison yard. At first he was puzzled because the youth had always checked in each day. Where could he be? Jim began looking more intently again in the nonrestricted areas. No one had seen him. He had just disappeared. Jim was sure that with all his informants he would have heard if there had been any foul play. He found himself heading for the chaplain's office to begin an official search. The next day Father Walsh informed Jim that Bill had been taken out of the population for "medical reasons" and that he would be back soon.

Three weeks later Bill appeared at the door of the chaplain's office. "What happened to you?" Jim asked in a loud, concerned voice as he pulled him into the office and closed the door.

"I had sort of a nervous breakdown," Bill replied.

"You don't just have a nervous breakdown all of a sudden without strugglin' with a lot of stuff before. What's been goin' on?"

Reaching inside to get the words out, Bill began to talk. "The reason I am in prison is that my twin sister and I thought we were in love with each other and we had sex. We couldn't get married but we lived together anyway. One day I wanted to get her a gift, but I didn't have any money so I robbed a store and got caught and got two to four years for it. So here I am. Since being here, I have not only been anxious and frightened at times concerning what could happen to me, but I've been realizing how I could have hurt or ruined my sister whom I love. I feel so ashamed. I just couldn't handle all this anymore."

As Jim pushed him against the wall, he yelled, "Why didn't you tell me about this?"

"I didn't want to," Bill yelled back, trying to read Jim's response, "because you would be ashamed of me and leave me."

Jim just stood there looking at him. Stunned, he replied slowly, "What could you ever say to me, of all people, that would shock me or make me so ashamed of you so that I would leave you?" More silence. "So this is why you have never asked me about the Third Order or why you never go to confession or communion, isn't it? Look at me!"

With his face reflecting inner anguish and conflict, Bill nodded. Then he added, "Don't you understand. I don't want to go in there to confession because God would never forgive me for what I've done."

With this Jim grabbed him by the collar, opened the door to Father Walsh's private office, and pushed Bill inside. Father Walsh was counseling another inmate, but Jim said, "Excuse us." And then he yelled to the other guy, "Get out." When the inmate left, Jim said to Father Walsh, "This young guy wants to go to confession. Take care of him right now." Jim closed the door and left. After Bill came out of Father's office, he said to Jim, "I am so happy—and free. I feel so good." Jim could see he was soaking in sweat, but he was relieved. He had a big grin on his face.

Later Father Walsh said, "You did a good thing, Jim, but if you ever barge into my office that way again, I'll kick your teeth through the back of your head. That's my office, not yours!"

Jim observed that Bill had become a changed man. *This friendship is really affectin' me. I feel so good inside, in my heart. I really love this kid, just like my son. This is what I'd want somebody to do if I had a son who was in trouble.*

Soon afterward, Bill's time was up and he left Rockview. It was a long time before Jim saw him again.

The Third Order of Saint Francis continued to grow, as did its demands for a greater commitment from Jim. Father Walsh turned the Order over to him. "You are going to be the one who gives the lessons and leads all the meetings," he said. The night before his first lesson, Jim was thinking about God's unconditional love toward him and the realization that he, in his lifetime, would never be able to comprehend it. In the concordance in the back of the Bible he looked up references to *love* and stumbled across 1 Corinthians 13—the "love chapter." He read it and a new realization exploded inside:

> Love is patient and kind; love is not jealous or boastful; it is not arrogant and rude. Love does not insist on its own way; it is not irritable or resentful; it does not rejoice at wrong but rejoices in the right. Love bears all things, believes all things, hopes all things, endures all things. Love never fails. (vv. 4–8)

In a meeting with Father Walsh the next day, Jim said, "Alice was what this passage said. I received all these things from Alice because, though initially for the wrong reasons, I was available to her. Love just snuck up on me. I was the recipient of this love from her. I am feeling great, great loss right now. I will never read this passage or think about it again without thinkin' about Alice and the loss and that I never at that time was capable of seein' it."

Jim was always trying to think of ways to make the Third Order lessons better and to maintain interest. For example, when the group participated in saying the Stations of the Cross during Lent, Jim said, "Let's pick fourteen guys and have each stand under one of the stations. When Father comes to the first station, he'll name it. Then the guy at that station will read the reflection and Father will read the prayer. We'll do that for each station." At first men volunteered just to have fun and goof around, but then some came back wanting to do it again. Jim didn't realize that these kinds of suggestions were a result of his growth as a leader.

At a Third Order meeting one night, Father Walsh and the brothers were sitting around talking about how they could improve the Saturday night service. Jim, who was sitting against the wall on top of a trashcan, suggested, "What we ought to do is cut out one of the two novenas to the Blessed Mother." At that moment the crucifix that hung on the wall above Jim fell, hit his head, and crashed to the floor. Father Walsh asked, "Has anyone anything else to suggest? Certainly at this moment the message is not to mess with the Blessed Mother!" Everyone discovered that God had a sense of humor!

The chaplain's office was a center of importance for the population at Rockview, and the Third Order of Saint Francis continued to deepen the lives of its members. Jim still met with new prisoners, but in addition to handing out material, he began to minister to their needs and tell them about the Lord's impact upon his life. His supportive and caring conversations continued with those awaiting counseling with Father Walsh and the other chaplains. Then one day Jim was informed that he was being given the Casey Martin Award. This award, named after a former prisoner, was given each year to Rockview's most outstanding Catholic in terms of service, ministry, and personal spiritual growth. At the celebration the bishop also officially installed Jim as the leader of the Third Order. When the ceremony concluded and the packed hall began to clear, Jim said, "Father, this is the first award I have ever received."

Father replied, "This award comes as a result of your fellow inmates' voting. It is in response to all you have done and all that the Lord has done in you. Have a great night's rest. I'll see you in the morning." After Father Walsh left, the guard who patrolled Jim's cell block each night came up to Jim. "Congratulations, Jim. I want to give you this book, which has meant a lot to me in my own life." As Jim took it, he had difficulty keeping eye contact because he remembered his early feelings about this guard.

"Thank you," Jim replied. "But I need to tell you somethin', and have needed to do so for a year now. From the moment I arrived here at Rockview until about a year ago when the Lord became real to me, I have wanted you dead, and I thought about ways that I could get you killed. I came here from Western hating guards and have hated you. I'd hear your footsteps echoing in the cellblock, then the silence as you stopped outside my cell, then the tapping of your billy club, and then the footsteps again. It used to make me so angry. I'd have awful thoughts about you, and I need right now to ask your forgiveness. Will you forgive me?"

"Jim," said the guard, " I do forgive you, but I also want you to know that I deal with a lot of things in my own life. I can never judge anyone because I believe that there but for the grace of God go I. I need a lot of prayer support and I am always aware that I need to be praying for others. Every night as I patrolled your cellblock, I was in continuous prayer, and when I stopped in front of each cell, I prayed for that inmate. When I got to your cell, I was always compelled to stay a little longer and pray a little more intently."

In a barely audible voice Jim replied, "I don't know what to say except 'thank you.' I guess I know right now that the changes in me have occurred more because of people like you than anything I have done. I am so grateful." In silence they parted and Jim headed for his cell, filled with amazement at how God works. That night he had a dream that brought even more significant change.

The next morning as he met with Father Walsh, Jim said, "As you know, Father, every night since Alice's murder I have had nightmares in which I have relived the horror and terror of that night. Last night, after that great celebration for me, I went to sleep and had another dream. Alice appeared to me and sat alongside my bed. She was sittin' there and smilin' at me. She sat there for a long time, and I felt she was tryin' to tell me something. I felt she was tellin' me she was at peace with the whole situation. Then a small child appeared and said, 'I love you, Daddy.' Father, I feel like it's all finally finished and I won't have to relive it anymore. If this is so, it doesn't mean that I won't think about them everyday. I can't imagin' ever comin' to that." After that night the nightmares ceased.

In adding the Casey Martin Award to Jim's files, Father Walsh realized that Jim had never submitted his commutation papers. In Pennsylvania, when one is given a life sentence, there is no maximum sentence. In other words, a life sentence can be commuted after twenty years. Father Walsh asked, "Why haven't you ever applied for commutation?"

Jim reminded him, "I'm not gonna, Father. I am in a good place in my life. As I've told you before, I believe I'm to stay in prison. That's where my ministry is and where I can best be used by God."

Father Walsh stated, "No, no, no, Jim. That's not the way it works. You put in your papers. If you're supposed to stay here, you'll stay." After more urging, Jim finally decided to enter the process and meet with the commutation board. The first meeting resulted in his being turned down because he had not served enough time. "After all," they said, "you are in here for first-degree murder." The second, third, and fourth meetings resulted in the same decision.

At this point Jim still believed that he was to stay in prison and that he no longer needed the truck job to escape, but as a result of these four meetings he could not deny his feelings that he would like to leave. Four refusals, however, began to affect his sense of hope of ever getting out and also began to create inner confusion. *Lord, what do you want me to do? What's happenin' here? I accept whatever you want.*

But Father Walsh continued to encourage him, and he applied for the fifth time. As he sat before the committee, he heard good reports from the guards of the cellblock. Father Walsh's description of his accomplishments in school and the warden's report on his outstanding maintenance work were also given. One of the impressive aspects of the meeting was that the board was made aware of the books Jim was reading and of his persistence as a student. Jim was dismissed from the meeting not believing things would be any different than in the past. Several days later he was taken to the D.W. Building (Death Waiting) to report to the psychologist. He entered the office. The psychologist was focused on the papers in front of him. He never looked up to greet Jim, but gestured for him to sit in the chair on the other side of the desk. Jim never liked sitting in silence in the presence of authority. It was all too reminiscent of the destructive pattern of his father. Jim grew increasingly uncomfortable.

The psychologist finally looked up from his papers and said, "Jim, you have your commutation. Your parole will start in two to three months." Reaching over his desk he extended his hand and said, "Congratulations." Jim sat down and tightly folded his arms across his abdomen to control what was happening inside. Observing Jim's body language, especially his eyes that were filling rapidly, the psychologist said, "Why don't I leave you alone for a bit. I'll be in the outer office. Just come out when you are ready."

Jim heard the door close behind him. His face fell into his hands. His arms could no longer keep back the sobs that seemed to rise from deep within him. When he finally became quiet, he went into the outer office where he was met by the captain of the guard and the deputy who in unison said, "God bless you, Jim." As he turned to leave, standing in the window of the chaplain's office next door was Father Walsh with his thumbs up, his face filled with joy. At that moment Jim realized that this was really going to happen!

On his last Sunday at Rockview, Jim was sitting up front in the chapel. The service had begun and he immersed himself in every minute, every hymn, and every prayer. From time to time he looked at the men around him, especially those brothers from the Third Order who had walked with him through so much change. These men would soon be walking him to the door through which he would go alone into his life ahead. Many he probably would never see again. Rockview had become holy ground, and in that sense, how could he ever leave it and the brothers who had so honored him with the Casey Martin Award? His eyes were filling up, and when Father Walsh began to preach, he thought, *How can I ever leave here without him?* At the conclusion of the sermon Father Walsh paused. Then he looked up and his eyes focused on Jim for a few moments. Finally he said, pointing to Jim, "This nut is going home next week. How do I say goodbye to a son?" *Oh Jesus,* Jim screamed inside, *Oh Jesus! Help me.*

Early the next morning Jim lay on his bunk, his body trying to wake up, his eyes not yet fully open, and his mind groping to get a handle on his feelings. *This is the day.*

Within hours I will be a free man. He couldn't fathom that he was not just leaving Rockview, he was leaving prison.

What time would they be calling him for his final meeting with the warden? *I better be ready*, he reflected. He rose quickly, shaved, showered, and went for breakfast. All he could handle was toast and coffee. Afterward he went to the D.W. Building where he exchanged his prison clothes for a suit, shirt, and tie—his "civilian" clothes. He then had to go back to his cellblock and wait for the call from the warden's office. Guards would come and escort him.

Time seemed to just hang there and he in suspension with it. These moments were filled with wonderment, anxiety, and fleeting seconds of excitement. Fellow inmates stopped by for final farewells along with guards he had known through the years. The phone rang frequently, but the guard would have a conversation with whomever, hang up, and then return to paperwork. More waiting. Finally the call came. The guard hung up and said, "OK, Jim, get outta here. It's time."

Soon two guards appeared at the door of the cellblock. "Lookin' pretty sharp, Jim. Are you ready?" They walked to the warden's office in the D.W. Building. The warden always had a meeting with inmates before they left. It was a time for Jim to say goodbye and to gain some last-minute advice. "Jim," the warden said, "after twenty years most everything will seem different. Don't be afraid. Take one day at a time. Don't make any compulsive decisions. Keep close and frequent connection with your parole officer for help and guidance." The warden then gave him the two hundred dollars he had earned. The warden shook his hand and said, "Good luck, Jim."

He was then taken to the main gate where Father Walsh was waiting in the car. The guards wished him well and at

9:00 a.m. on June 19, 1967, the car pulled away and headed down the long driveway flanked by wide lawns and flowerbeds. Inmate friends of Jim's were working on the grounds and they waved as his car passed. Looking back at them, Jim caught a final glimpse of the D.W. Building commanding the countryside, the high razor-wire fencing connected to it and encasing the compound of brick cell blocks behind it. As the car left the drive and headed down the main road, Father Walsh said, "Jim, we are now off prison property and you are a free man." His words penetrated Jim's deepest area of disbelief that he would ever get out of prison. He was overcome with joy. They drove in silence down Rt. 220 to Father Walsh's house in Tyrone, Pennsylvania. There they spent time before lunch discussing Jim's expectations for the future and the things that he needed to do upon his arrival in Pittsburgh. Suddenly Father Walsh looked at his watch and announced that it was time to go to lunch.

The owner of the restaurant where they went recognized Father Walsh immediately and knew that he was bringing Jim for his first meal outside the prison. Father Walsh and the restaurant owner had talked prior to this occasion and were wondering what Jim would order. They guessed wrong. He ordered fried chicken with mashed potatoes and gravy. "Welcome, Jim," the owner said, greeting him. "We all have heard about today. Congratulations. Your lunch is on me." There was a Jewish man eating close enough to overhear the conversation, and he said, "I'm going to fill out this prayer slip and put it in a special box in my synagogue where it will be taken out at certain times. You need to know that we will be praying for you, and this request will always be in our midst."

When lunch was over and final congratulations were extended, Father Walsh drove to the Tyrone depot where Jim was to board the train for Pittsburgh. They stood on the platform beside the train for the remaining few minutes before it departed. Steam could be seen and heard escaping from the break connections between the coaches. Large clouds of hissing steam also came out from under the engine several cars away.

"Jim," said Father Walsh, "here is fifty dollars. I want you to take it just in case. And I want you to promise that if you ever need anything, you will call me. Do you promise?"

Jim responded with a nod and said, "Yes, I promise." The conductor, holding onto the stair rail and with one foot already on the first stair of the car, yelled, "All aboard!" The two men stood there. They shook hands, looking at each other. There were now no words that could ever describe what they had shared together through the years. The train gave a start and began to roll ever so slowly. Jim stepped onto the first riser, grabbed the handrail, and turned quickly to wave good bye, but Father Walsh was gone. *Oh Lord, this hurts so bad!*

The train was picking up speed as he finished climbing the stairs. He entered the coach and found a seat. Suddenly he was engulfed in a frightening awareness. *I am really on my own. Oh Jesus, help me!* He moved to find a seat next to a window. It was hard to focus on the scenery with all of the thoughts and feelings and concerns roaming around inside him.

"Tickets!"

Startled, Jim was unaware that the conductor had come up to his seat and he looked at the man without understanding what was happening. The conductor said, "Sir, may I have your ticket, please." It had been years since Jim had ridden a train, and it took a minute for him to finally realize that he had to give the conductor his ticket. Fumbling around in his suit pockets, he finally found it, handed it to the conductor, and then watched as the man took his puncher and clicked holes in certain places on the ticket before tearing off the end and handing it back.

Jim's attention now shifted to looking out the train window. *Look at all those cars. There are so many on the road. They look so different. They're goin' so fast. What am I gonna do for a job? Where will I look? What about clothes? What is that guy wearin' across the aisle? Where is my family? How will I ever make contact? Are they even alive?*

Between all his anxious questions and looking out the window of the train, the trip went quickly. As the train pulled into Penn Station in Pittsburgh, a church came into his view through the window. *The first thing I'm gonna do is go to that church,* Jim thought. He went in and sat for awhile, giving thanks for all the blessings of the day. Then he walked to a taxi that took him to a halfway house, "Parting of the Ways," his new home. The staff was waiting for his arrival and showed him to his room. Jim sat down on the bed and that's the last thing he remembered of that day.

In this halfway house, job-search meetings were held for the residents. A request from a cleaning company was presented at one of the meetings, and Jim went out that day, interviewed, and got the job. Work started two days later. He decided that on his free day he was going to the movies. As he bought his ticket, he remembered the train ticket incident. Following the movie, he went to several restaurants to get a cup of coffee and something to eat, but mainly to look at people and try to overhear what they were talking about. Strolling through department stores was part of the afternoon agenda as well. Things were so expensive. In the days that followed, Jim spent his free time just walking around town looking and listening.

Jim soon moved from the halfway house to Saint Joseph's House of Hospitality on Tannahill Street in the Hill district of Pittsburgh. There he did maintenance work and odd jobs and eventually moved to a small apartment. He wished for something different and didn't realize that a wonderful opportunity was about to happen. While at Rockview Jim had become part of the Holy Name Society and was contacted to continue working with the Society on the outside. In the Society he met Mr. Wolfenberger who took Jim under his wing in many areas of his new life and helped him reenter society. Together they ministered in different areas of the city—to alcoholics, to patients at Kane Hospital who were formerly in prison, and to former prisoners now in residence at Saint Joseph's House of Hospitality, to mention a few.

One day Mr. Wolfenberger took Jim to Dormont, a suburb of Pittsburgh, to visit the Donahue family whose son was having some difficulties. Jim was told it would be of help to Mr. Wolfenberger if he would talk with the son. When the appointment was over, Mrs. Donahue (Betty) stated that they had a beautiful apartment upstairs and said that if Jim ever heard of anyone who needed one to let her know. He said, "How much is it?" She said, "Eighty dollars a month." Jim asked if he could rent it. The answer was "yes" and he moved in. After a few weeks he realized that his work schedule and the need to use public transportation were making it difficult to find places to eat dinner. Since he didn't know how to cook, he asked Betty Donahue if he could pay for his own food but eat dinner at her home. An arrangement was made for Jim to eat dinner in their home, but the way he could pay back the Donahues was on payday to buy a meal for the whole family.

It wasn't long before he found that he had a significant role in the life of this family of twelve. Mr. Donahue was basically a loner. After dinner at night he would leave the table and go to his room. He had little connection with the children, and thus Betty became the father as well as the mother, disciplining, getting the kids to church, making them do their chores and schoolwork, and so on. Jim, by his presence and strength, was becoming the dominant male influence in the family. In his interaction with the kids he was positive, supportive, strict, and compassionate. For Betty he became a confidant and mentor. The Donahues became Jim's family and they all grew together with a deep affection for each other.

Having reentered the "real world," Jim realized one day that he needed to open a bank account. He went into a bank to do so, and the teller said, "Yes sir. How much do you want to start with?" Jim had $180.00. The teller asked, "May I ask what kind of work you do?" Jim replied, "Well, I am doin' odd jobs right now. You see I just came out of prison after twenty years. I'd rather tell you this now. If you feel this would be an embarrassment, no hard feelins." The teller said, "No, that's fine."

It seemed to Jim, however, as if he had to relearn everything in terms of simple daily living. Crossing a street was frightening. He couldn't judge how fast cars were going or estimate how much time he had to get across. One night his timing was off and he was almost hit head on by a car. Not only did cars move faster than they did twenty years earlier, but also there were more of them. He needed to become aware of such changes and practice new skills, even simple ones like crossing a street.

He also had to relearn the value of certain merchandise such as clothing. He didn't know how to select wisely in terms of the kind of clothing he needed. He wanted to look "cool," but how to choose a suit and the right tie and shoes was confounding. He didn't know how much he should spend or how to work out a payment plan that would make certain things he needed more available to him. He had to learn how much to tip in a restaurant. He had to learn how to figure out bus schedules in order to get to work on time and get back home for a 6 p.m. dinner at the Donahue's. Laundry had to be done. By 10 p.m. he had great difficulty staying awake even if he needed to. He realized that twenty years of enforced lights-out at 10 p.m. was not going to be changed overnight. He was exhausted dealing with all these new things.

During one of their meetings Mr. Wolfenberger mentioned to Jim that he was going on a short trip to Bethlehem, Pennsylvania. Jim said he had a cousin who used to be a priest in Bethlehem. "What's his name?" asked Mr. Wolfenberger. "Father Leonard Townsend." "I know him," was the reply. "I'll have him come here and meet with you."

When his cousin Father Leonard came, he told Jim all about his family. "What family?" asked Jim. "I thought they all were dead. My father came to visit me soon after I got to Western and never visited me again. I wrote letters to him but he never answered them. Also, my brother Fran forwarded to me an insurance policy renewal notice, which I let go, but I never heard nothin' from him again either."

"Jim, I know where to contact your brother Fran and sister Marie. Leave this up to me." Instead of being enraged and resentful in getting the news that his family was still alive, Jim was overjoyed. Outside of his father and Fran's one visit, no one had ever made contact with him during his twenty years in prison, and he had just assumed they were all dead. Now he discovered that he still had family and was no longer totally alone. He eagerly looked forward to seeing them because of the deep forgiveness he had recently experienced. Whatever the reasons they didn't contact him, he could harbor no resentments and anger.

Soon Jim was on his way to Bethlehem with his cousin Father Leonard to see his brother Fran and his family. It was an emotional reunion, as Fran expressed his joy that things had turned out so well for Jim. Jim discovered that Fran had become a decorated World War II hero. He had done well in his career, but was in constant pain from wounds that wouldn't heal.

Father Leonard next made contact with Marie who in turn phoned Jim that she was coming from Philadelphia to see him. Soon after her arrival, Jim discovered that the bond they both had known was still there, the bond that had deepened when their mother died and Marie had to run the household. They held each other and cried. The flood that poured out of Jim's heart washed away his belief that he was totally alone in this world. Marie told Jim that she was the mother of twelve children and was married to a very physically abusive, alcoholic husband. She had been trapped in her marriage, and there was no way she could have come to see Jim. She also had no emotional energy to deal with anything except her own survival. Jim also found out that his sister Ann had indeed become a recluse, whom no one had seen since their mother's funeral.

Soon after this visit Marie made arrangements to pick Jim up one day. When they were in the car she said, "I'm taking you to see Bob." While on their way Marie told Jim of conversations she had had with their brother Fran. "Jim," she said, "Fran and I have realized that after Mom died there were a lot of things we did wrong. We want you to know that if we had done some things differently, you probably wouldn't have had to go through all that you did. We are so sorry. You know, after our father came to visit you at

Western, he made a proclamation that your name was never to be mentioned again in the family. We're also sorry that we listened to that and we're also sorry that we didn't write to you. Now we are going to see Bob. Are you ready?" *The hurt from the wound Bob gave me is still there,* Jim thought as Marie parked in front of Bob's house.

Bob's wife opened the door and led Jim to the living room where Bob was waiting for him. The two brothers stood there looking at each other. Bob was visibly frightened. At that moment Jim remembered the time Bob had set him up to be arrested for pulling the fire alarm box when he, Bob, had actually done it. Because of that incident Jim had been sent to Glen Mills reform school. He thought of his parting words to Bob: *"I'll be out some day, and when I get out, I'll beat you near to death." Bob remembers those words too. Look at him—he is afraid of me, knowin' that I served time for a murder rap.*

No words were exchanged as the two men searchingly looked at each other, trying to determine what each one was feeling and thinking. Finally Bob said, "I want to tell you something. Let's go into the other room." Bob closed the door and said, "I'm really glad to see you again."

Jim replied, "I know that."

Bob said, "I've never seen you as mad as you were that day at Glen Mills. Please don't hate me for what I did. I am so sorry and have been sorry for a long time. I want us to be friends."

In full awareness of the forgiveness he had received in his own life as well as the healing of painful memories, Jim replied, "I don't hate you, Bob. I guess I never really did. Crazy as it sounds, in spite of all the problems and pain you caused, you were the only real companion I ever had. We were and are still brothers."

As they stood looking at each other, they began to cry, the unresolved loss and pain and grief that had accumulated over the years now being freely expressed. They both needed support at that moment, physically and emotionally. Hesitatingly but almost simultaneously, they began to raise their arms toward each other. After a few awkward steps they finally reached each other in an embrace that would establish the beginning of the healing process between them. They seemed to be there for an eternity as neither wanted to let go of the other. Later Bob's wife, Elaine, said, "Jim, take a look at Bob's prayer book. Yes, that's your picture in there. It always has been there." *If only I had known this,* Jim thought.

Months later Elaine said, "You know, Jim, you and Bob are so different. He's really a good husband, but he's quiet. However, when you come to visit, you two do more talking than he and I do in ten days. I can't believe it." By the time Bob moved to Florida because of deteriorating health, the reconciliation between the brothers was complete and they continued to communicate with each other across the miles.

While Jim continued to do maintenance work at Saint Joseph's House of Hospitality, along with other odd jobs, his involvement with the Holy Name Society deepened. Jim seemed to have an increasing desire for ministry to the extent that it dominated much of his thinking and prayer time. One Sunday at Saint Bernard's, where Jim attended church, he was talking with a fellow parishioner about his increasing desire to enter the fulltime ministry, and he added that he had been thinking about the Trappists and the Gethsemani Trappist Monastery in Louisville, Kentucky.

"Jim," asked the parishioner, "have you thought of investigating the Capuchin Franciscan Order?"

Jim's responded, "Who are they? I never heard of them." The parishioner stated that he had a son who was a

Capuchin priest and gave him his son's phone number to call if he was interested. Jim phoned but was referred to the Capuchin vocational director, Father Lester Knoll. After many attempts he finally connected with Father Lester and set up an appointment. One of Jim's co-workers drove him to that first meeting at Saint Augustine's parish. For all subsequent meetings Jim took public transportation.

Father Lester was intrigued with Jim, but his history raised many red flags regarding the possibility of his candidacy. Whether in Father Lester's office, on the long walks they took, or in subsequent telephone conversations, Jim's healing process, his psychological tests, the requirements of a Capuchin, and the nature of their purpose in the world were crucial topics in their discussions together. Also central in their discussions was Jim's wrestling with his desire to be a Trappist monk.

"The Trappists have had a powerful ministry through the years, but why do you want to become one?" Father Lester asked.

Jim always seemed to come back to the same reasoning: "I have been such a destructive sinner. I could really give my life to God behind those walls at Gethsemani and be a part of that prayerful community."

Father Lester would, in so many words, complete Jim's thinking, saying "Yes, you'd be in this marvelous place behind those walls beating yourself up further for the rest of your life because you are so rotten, under the guise of doing penance." As Jim remained silent, Father Lester continued, "Jim, as forgiven people we are to surrender ourselves as we are to the Lord, gifts and warts and all, for him to use for his honor and glory in the world. You're not to spend your life burying yourself in a Trappist monastery. With your personality, you need people and an active ministry. As a Capuchin you will spend much time in prayer, but have time for ministry in the world."

With the interviewing process completed, Father Lester told Jim that he had to meet with the other priests and brothers and review all of the information covered. A decision would be made and Jim would be notified. "If you are accepted, Jim," said Father Lester, "it will be to come to the community at Saint Francis Friary as an associate member for a year, which will serve as your postulancy, that is, your probationary period as a candidate for membership in the Capuchin Order. An associate member is a new status whereby a layman such as yourself lives and fully participates in the community life and its disciplines while still doing a full-time secular job. At the conclusion of a year, you and we would review your readiness to enter the order beginning as a novice."

A week later Father Lester arrived at the Donahue's home and asked Jim, "How does November 28 sound to you?"

"For what?" Jim asked.

"That's when I will come and pick you up and take you to the Friary. Are you ready?" Jim's whole body said, "Yes." In the days that followed, he began the process of divesting himself of all of his possessions, including bank accounts, record player, and the like. It was required of one making a solemn profession. The day he was picked up, all he would have would be the clothes on his back and a few other necessary articles.

The week before Jim left the Donahue's to enter the Friary, he received an urgent message from his cousin Father Leonard telling him that his father was dying. "I am coming to pick you up and take you to the hospital in Philadelphia," Father Leonard said. *How am I gonna get through this visit? I can't forget hearin' about him tellin' everyone that my name was never to be mentioned again in his house after his visit with me at Western. You never answered my letters. Am I gonna get shut out again? Oh, I don't want to be goin' through all of these thoughts—Dad, you pushin' me into the Marines, dumpin' me into an orphanage after Mom died, always favorin' Bob, your meanness comin' out of the booze, never wonderin' where I was, ridin' the rails. But then you always took care of Mom during her sickness, you never left the house without bein' sure she was OK. You always kept the house clean, you never let Bob and me go out at night—so Mom wouldn't worry. We got the strap when we screwed up.*

Jim continued to reflect upon the tough life his father had making his way, working on the railroad and ranches out west herding cattle, working in coal mines. He had to be tough to make it. He worked hard. Nobody messed with him. If they did, they never did it again. He lost everything during the Depression. He was a bitter man. He never trusted banks again. He worked hard and succeeded in paying off all the debt from his wife's illness.

Jim arrived at the hospital and his brothers and sisters were there. During the visit Jim asked if he could shave his father, and the nurse said, "Well, we don't have priests going around shaving too many patients." Jim's father said, "This isn't a priest, this is my son, and he is a monk." Deep down inside Jim asked, *What did he say? He said, "This is my son....This is my son." This is the first time he ever said that I belonged to him. Oh God, I can't believe it.*

Marie interrupted his thoughts, turning to him and in a whisper saying, "Jim, you should have been where I was standing when he turned to the nurse and made that statement. You should have seen his eyes light up and the expression on his face." Jim's internal response was, *I know now that we have become father and son. I know it!*

A few days after he returned to the Donahue's, Betty told him that his father had died. When he returned to Philadelphia for the funeral, Marie said, "Jim, I'm going to tell you something I have never told anyone else. Every day when Dad said his Rosary, I was in earshot and every day, for twenty years, he remembered you in the Rosary. I heard him. Even though he made that statement to never mention your name again, Jim, you were always there."

The deprived feelings of a lifetime rushed forward to savor these words and ingest their love-giving nourishment. *I finally now know where his heart was.*

Patrick Townsend died on November 19, 1970. He was eighty-four years old. Jim attended his funeral in Bethlehem, Pennsylvania, on November 25. Three days later, on the first day of Advent, he would take his first step in becoming a Capuchin Brother by taking up residence at Saint Francis Friary.

CHAPTER 9

The Postulancy

The whole Donahue family was lined up at the door as Jim was getting ready to leave. Little Matt said, "We ain't never going to see him again, are we?" All assured him that Jim would be back for visits. Jim said to Paula, the Donahue's daughter, "God, honey, I love you and Matt so much. You let me come to your home, and you were never afraid of me." Paula responded, "No, never!"

The whole family followed Jim as he headed for Father Lester's car. They stood at the curb in front of their house and tearfully waved good-bye as the car pulled out into traffic, taking Jim to the beginning of his new life at Saint Francis Friary. Jim stuck his arm out of the window and waved, looking back at them until Father Lester turned the corner at the end of the street, and they disappeared from sight. Jim was silent for awhile. It was obvious to Father Lester that he was struggling with the closing of this chapter in his life, knowing how much he loved the Donahue family and they loved him.

There was no yellin' or fightin'. They just took me as I was and made me part of their family. I'm gonna miss them. Jim needed his handkerchief. His sadness was interrupted as they drove through areas of the city that had changed. He saw many new things that reminded him of Saint Paul's writing in Second Corinthians—all things becoming new. Father Lester eventually broke into the silence and asked, "Is there

131

anything going on with you this moment that you'd like to talk about?"

"Yeah," Jim replied. "I've been thinkin' about a lot of things." As he started talking, the thoughts began pouring out. "I've been thinkin' about the Donahues and how nice they were to me and how they became my family and how much I'm gonna miss them. But I've also been thinkin' about all things bein' new. You know Saint Paul was a tough guy. He went through a lot of pain too. He was in the slammer in Rome and them prisons were lousy! Caesar locked him up. But before that, he was in Corinth and saw all the wild stuff goin' on there, and when he got home, he wrote them a letter.

"In Second Corinthians he's talkin' to them about what they can experience in Christ. He says somethin' like 'If anybody is in Christ he is new—a new creature. Old things have passed away, all things become new.' Yeah, this is what's been happenin' to me. Ya know, since wakin' up that morning in Rockview and sayin', 'God, you're real,' it's like I've been hearin' the Lord sayin' to me through the years, 'Hey, Jimmy, I've waited a long time for us to be with each other like now.' The other day, Father, when you called this a mystical union I had to go look up the word *mystical*. What do you know, the dictionary even had it right. I learned that it means that 'God can be known directly.' Yeah! This I know. It's deep. Ya know, if we're close to a person, we can experience somethin' like this with them—a deep connection. I certainly knew this with Alice. So, we can know this with God.

"So I'm feelin' the Lord sayin', 'Jimmy, when I'm talkin' about a guy in Christ, I'm talkin' about change. I'm not talkin' about gettin' yourself cleaned up. You stopped fightin' and cussin' and doin' stuff like that. If you're doin' good with it all, it's because of what's way down inside.' Father, you said that it's a radical change. Like I'm hearin' the Lord sayin, 'This is what I'm doin' in you. You're not the same!'

"I guess what really gets to me is when Paul is talkin' about the old passin' away. I never saw beyond the old. I remember sayin' my whole life, 'Jim takes care of Jim.' I always felt like no one ever took care of me. What was important was what was gonna help me be safe, no matter what the cost. Until Alice, I never really thought of helpin' others or bein' close and stuff like that. Certainly there was none of that in *my* family except maybe for Marie. But ya know, I've felt the Lord sayin', 'I've used all your hurt and pain and lostness to bring us together.' After that happened, all things started to become new. What gets me is why God even wanted to bother with me!

"I feel like the blind man in the Gospels. He was born blind. So Jesus healed him, and then the Pharisees came to him and asked, 'Hey, how come you're seein'?' They were out to get Jesus' butt for healin' on the Sabbath. So this blind guy says, 'I don't know. Yesterday I was blind, but now I'm seein'. I don't know.' Here's what really gets me. I know that with all these changes that I must really be loved, but I don't deserve nothin'. Now, Father, this is the kind of thinkin' I've been doin'.'"

"Jim," Father responded, "you've begun your postulancy!"

The car entered the Brookline section of Pittsburgh and turned onto Castlegate Avenue, driving along the expansive property known as the Toner Institute, which was an orphanage for homeless boys run by the Sisters of Divine Providence. The Capuchins were the chaplains for the Institute and lived at the Friary, located at the edge of the property. Father Lester slowly pulled up in front of the Friary, giving Jim an opportunity to view his new home. It was a three-story Gothic English manor-like structure with gables. The façade was done in the beautiful gray Belgian block seen often in Pittsburgh. Jim felt that it looked more like a sanctuary than a fortress.

The large heavy oak entrance door opened into a narrow corridor where Father Lester introduced Jim to Father Myles Schmidt and Father Bill Wiethorn who, excited about their new colleague, took Jim on a tour of the friary. Jim saw the visiting rooms off the corridor and then the very intimate stained-glass-windowed chapel. Its focal point was a large crucifix, a replica of one carved in the 1600s that was done by one of the priests. Across from the chapel was the door of the friary. They entered into a dimly lit hall. Jim looked at a community bulletin board with all the notices that would be affecting his day. The staircase next to the bulletin board took him up to his room. It was small, sparkling clean, and simple, with a coat cupboard, desk, chair, and bed. A small window looked out on Castlegate Avenue, but did not allow the noise of the street to invade upon the magnificent quiet that filled the room. Jim sat on his bed and the peace of the room invaded his whole body.

Prior to leaving the Donahue's, Jim had been employed by the Tome Maintenance and Cleaning Company of Pittsburgh. His work was waiting for him the next morning as he awakened for the first time in the castle that housed him and his new community. This day marked the beginning of maintaining a full-time job while entering into and sharing the life of the community at the friary. At the evening meal with the priests and brothers, someone asked Jim how he had gotten this job having so recently been released from prison.

"I will never forget how I got my job at Tome's," Jim replied, conveying a deep sense of deep gratitude through his words. "It was a guy I knew when I was livin' at Saint Joseph's House of Hospitality in the Hill District who told me about this job. So I went out there for an interview. The man knew that I could do floors, run the buffer, repair stuff, and do all kinds of other maintenance jobs. So he hired me. But first he went to the man I was gonna be workin' with, and he didn't realize that I could hear their conversation through the vent system. What I heard was one of them things that stays with you for the rest of your life.

"He says, 'John, I'm thinkin' of hirin' a fellow. He's the kind of guy we really need and he'd be workin' with you. I have to tell you he just got out of prison. He did a life sentence. He had a murder charge on him.' And John said, 'Well, you know, if he doesn't get a chance, how can he prove himself?' And from that moment on we were the best of friends. When we were introduced, he said, 'Hi, Jim. Call me John.' We were a twosome from then on.

"Ya know, as I began to get into this job before comin' here, I began to make some discoveries about myself pretty quick. I saw some new things. I wanted to have fun. I wanted to help people laugh. I wanted to do little things for people. I remember John and me were doin' this office and the boss came out and because of some scheduling problems he stopped us from doin' our work. So we went and made signs sayin', 'The boss won't let us work.' Everybody in the office about cracked up and said, 'We heard of strikes before, but this is the first time we heard of someone mad at the boss 'cause he wouldn't let him work.' Ya know, little things like this make a difference to people."

Each evening the community of priests and brothers listened and watched with great interest as Jim spoke of reentering society and accepting the responsibilities put on him in a daily work environment. At the table one evening the guardian asked Jim, "How was the day?" Jim answered, "There was this young girl who just turned twenty-one so

me and John went and got her a birthday cake and left it for
her. When we went back a month later to clean again, they
all said, 'Oh, you should have been here when she came in
and saw the cake. She couldn't believe it. And we all had a
little party.' Ya know, it's little things like that that make ya
feel good. I remember one time me and John had to go to
Jew Street, named because mostly Jewish people lived there.
Wow! They had perfect homes, in good shape, like the grass
was cut, and there were flowers and all that stuff.

"At this one home I always began [cleaning] at this one
window. One day when I got up there at the top of the ladder, this lady scared the life out of me 'cause she was starin'
out the window at me and was waitin' for me. She opened
the window and said, 'You know something, Jim. You've
been coming here for about six months now and I know
about you. Your boss had to tell us.' I said, 'That's OK. I
never held nothin' back.' She said, 'I was waiting here
because I wanted to tell you something. You know, if we had
to do it all over again, I wish my husband had a job like
yours. Look at this house. It's a big house. He always made
a big salary. Now he's in that bed up there, a cripple. Because
he worked so many hours, one day he woke up and couldn't
move. We're well to do. The kids are OK, but we don't have
a life any more. Now, I watch you two out there. You don't
have much, but I don't think I've ever seen a day, regardless
of the weather, when you two aren't laughing. And my kids
love it when you come here. You did my daughter's play-
house. She gave you two dollars to do her windows and you
gave the money back to me and I'd keep it in an envelope till
the next time. She didn't know it was the same two dollars.'
We laughed. 'My daughter had to learn to make sure you got
paid.' Guys," Jim told his community that evening, "it's
things like this that was just fantastic for me.

"I remember one house we stopped at. I noticed that the lady looked down and out. I said, 'My gosh, lady, about the only thing left for you is a tombstone!' 'Oh,' she said, 'I'm telling you. Are you married?' I said, 'No.' She said, 'Well, stay that way. Kids are crazy today.' I said, 'Oh, yeah? What happened?' She said, 'My kid doesn't want to go to school and grow up and be like me. Yeah, I'm always working. I never have time to go out and build snowmen and that kind of thing.'

"'OK,' I said. 'One of these days when I get back here, we'll have a little talk.' I eventually did have the privilege of meetin' the child. She was six and a half years old. I started to kid her. I said, 'Listen, I've been thinkin'. I'm kinda lonely sometimes. Would you marry me?' She ran and said, 'Mom, I just got proposed to.' Her mom said, 'Are you going to leave me?' And she said, 'No, mom, I wouldn't leave you, but there's something just not right here.'"

Everyone laughed. "Jim, what was important to you in this situation?" one of the brothers asked.

"Well," Jim replied, "I felt it helped her to know who was most important to her. Ya know, I just sensed that this little girl could use a laugh since there was no father around. I told a guy once that I made up my mind I was gonna just make people laugh. Somehow they feel better when they can laugh. Wow! How did I ever get to this place? It's hard to believe that this is the kind of stuff that excites me. I remember one time I was at a 'mission' at Rockview just before gettin' out. The prison warden said, 'I got some letters about you.' I said, 'Oh, yeah? What's up?' He said, 'Guys wrote and said that the only reason they made it was on account of you. You first of all took the time to be with them. But then you told them things they needed to hear, like not to worry about how much money they got or where they were gonna live, that it was how they lived that counted. Because, you said, the day you stand before God, He's not gonna ask you how much money you got, but what you did for him. That's the question that determines your life.' The warden told me these men really heard that."

Jim drew his sharing time to a close by stating, "During my last days in prison what I was realizin' more and more is that I did them things not because I had to or, like in the old days, 'cause it would get me the truck job at Rockview. But I did them 'cause deep down I wanted to. Amazin', ain't it?"

One day the cleaning company boss referred Jim and John to a special job. "We went to visit a prospective client," Jim told his community at dinner. "He asked us, 'Do you do extra work?' I said, 'Yeah.' The client asked, 'Would you wash down my house. I've done it every year for twelve years and then I paint it. Now I'm getting a little old to do this. I'll give you five bucks an hour.' Just then a kinda grumpy neighbor came out and says, 'What are you guys doing?' The owner said, 'I'm gonna get my house fixed up.' The neighbor said, 'You're always painting that thing.' He then went into his house. He didn't know that we were just going to wash it. So we got the scaffolding up and I did the whole side of the house before noon. Now, I'm restin' a bit before doin' the rest of the house, and this neighbor comes out and says, 'You know, I seen people paint before, but I ain't seen anybody paint that fast.' I decided to have some fun with him and told him this was the new speed-dryin' paint. 'Oh, yeah,' he says. I finished the house and was ready to leave and the guy comes out and gets in my face and says, 'Wise guy. I found out.' We got some real laughin' goin' and everybody started feelin' good."

Upon returning to the friary each day, Jim went directly to the chapel to give thanks. He would then clean up and take a rest. Each week Jim gave Father Lester part of his paycheck to help support the community. If there was any work to be done around the house, Jim did it. Sometimes at night he went out to see certain people and minister to their needs or he'd go with Father Lester to a prayer group. He was well-integrated into the daily life of the community at the friary that involved morning and evening prayer, house chapter meetings, and time for conversation, for deepening his spiritual life, and for periods of reflection with Father Myles Schmitt, his confessor.

In the new life that was evolving, a much-anticipated time of the week was Sunday. When Sundays came, Jim went to Kane Hospital, which he had been doing with Mr. Wolfenburger and the Holy Name Society since his release from prison. He quickly made friends with a lot of the staff and patients. "One of the funny things that happened the first time I went there," he told Father Lester, "was when I went into this one room. I had my collar on. There was a lady [patient] there that was big breasted and she would bare her breasts whenever a guy came into the room, which would embarrass everyone. When I walked in, she did just that. I looked and said, 'Well, it's not quite like Marilyn Monroe's, but not too bad!' Then I went over to the person I had come to see and later left the room. The nurse ran up to me and says, 'Oh, Father, I'm so sorry. I meant to warn you.' 'No problem,' I said. The next week when I went there, the nurse says, 'Well, you cured her!' I said, 'How did I do that?' She answered. 'She doesn't do it anymore 'cause you insulted her!'

"Well, this lady wouldn't talk to me for a long time. I went by her room one day to pray with some people next door and she yelled out, 'Hey, how come you don't come in and see us no more?' I walked in and said, 'What's up?' And she said, 'Does there have to be anything up?' And I said, 'Know that you still look beautiful.' And she told me to drop dead. But you know that's what really started us off. We would yak about stuff. Then one day she told me about her son just walkin' out and she said, 'I'd be a liar if I told you it don't hurt. I keep hoping that maybe one day he'll show up.' Funny thing about mothers, they never stop bein' a mother just because their kids go off somewhere. 'Just pray for him every day,' I said. 'Maybe he will show up.' I don't know if he ever did, but that conversation led me to a lady next to her one day.

"This lady was really complainin' and she said, 'Father, if God's so great, why do I suffer like this?' I said, 'I haven't the slightest idea. But ya know, if you read the scriptures, you'll find if you put your suffering on the cross and pray for others in their pain, it may not take your pain away, but you'll save a lot of souls in purgatory. I believe prayin' for all these people in their pain really changes things for them and it changes you. Maybe you know someone who needs a blessin' or somethin' like that.'

"One of the most beautiful things I ever heard was one Sunday a couple of weeks later when one of these ladies said, 'Well, Jim, we must have got a lot of people out of purgatory this week 'cause we all really hurt.' How about that! A little ministry got started. Hey, Saint Paul says of Jesus, 'I make all things new.'"

After Jim was at the friary for about a year, he knew that he wanted to become a brother. It was also clear to him that the best way to use his talents and serve the Lord was not behind the walls of a Trappist monastery, as he had first wanted, but rather by following the Capuchin Franciscan discipline that blends the contemplative and active way of life. He told his superior that he would like to enter the novitiate and begin training at Saint Conrad's Friary in Annapolis, Maryland.

Would his request be granted?

CHAPTER 10

All Things Become New

Jim had spent a successful year as a postulant, experiencing a variety of ministry opportunities in Pittsburgh, and growing in his relationships in the Capuchin community, all the while working in his secular job at the cleaning company. Becoming a novice would be the next step in the process of his becoming a brother. His request was voted on during a meeting that included all the brothers and priests of the community of Saint Francis Friary. Their answer was unanimous: *Yes!*

Along with other novices, Jim was soon taken to Alverno Retreat Center for a week of orientation, getting acquainted, work, and prayer. The disciplined life began immediately. Mass and then breakfast and a work period followed an early rising. A midday prayer period took place before lunch, followed by a time of quiet and solitude. A recreational period proceeded supper, which was followed by evening prayer. Then the novices would gather to talk about the day and to process what had happened individually and in community.

At the end of their week at Alverno, the novices were taken to Saint Conrad's Friary in Annapolis where they immediately entered into an eight-day retreat. At the conclusion of this week was a service of investiture at which the novice received his brown-hooded habit, modeled after the one worn by Saint Francis. Putting on the habit and securing the waist with the cord tied with three knots, symbolizing the vows of poverty, chastity, and obedience, profoundly moved Jim. This habit also symbolized the words of Saint Paul, "Putting off the old man and putting on the new." His mind flashed back to his experiences with the brothers at Saint Francis Orphanage. He smiled when he thought, *I wonder what they would think if they could see me now.*

Following this investiture came a year of basic spiritual formation that included the study of the life of Saint Francis and of the *Constitutions of Capuchin Friars,* and prayer. Overseeing and caring for the welfare of the novices was their guardian, Father John Getsy. One day, after Jim had been there several months, Father John asked him, "What's happening to you? What are you learning?"

"Father," Jim responded, "there has been an ongoin' thought that is present in whatever I'm doin'. Saint Paul says, 'Behold the old has passed away, all things become new.' So much continues to become new for me. What started in prison in my maintenance work has taken on new meanin' as I am lookin' at the new teachin' about doin' work and seein' my work and myself in it all.

"Father, the big shots, and probably a lot of other kinds of people, might look at me like I'm not doin' nothin' important enough. Yeah, I didn't have much education, and I ain't gonna ever be worth much to most people, but what I do in fixin' and cleanin' is not nothin'!

"Let me show you what it says in the *Constitutions of the Capuchin Friars.* It says important stuff to me. These are the parts I really connect with." And Jim read,

Each one of us according to each one's capacity and God's spiritual gifts is suited for different kinds of work....Let the work of each brother be an expression of the entire fraternity. Let each one according to his

God-given talents and the condition of his age and health make full use of his energies with joy, keeping in mind the needs of the fraternity ["for me at this point," Jim added, "this included all people"]. We should always keep in mind our apostolic calling so that in any activity we may offer to people a witness to Christ.

"This is havin' a clearer meanin' for me with a sense of God bein' with me as I work and as I look at what I did before.

"Ya know, when I was buffin' floors, paintin', fixin', and things like that, the Lord was in me 'cause I had asked him into my life in prison. But I'm realizin' with him bein' in me, he was also in the middle of what I was doin'. I wouldn't have been where I was and doin' them floors and stuff if it wasn't for him. In prison I'd find myself prayin' and thankin' him. Like, I'd find myself prayin' when I passed the Stations of the Cross in the chapel doin' floors. Or when I was workin', I'd get ideas, certain kinds of thoughts, that I would put into a talk or teachin'. Or I'd say the Rosary. Or, just workin' there by myself I'd listen for the Lord to speak to me some way, bein' there with him, doin' what he's given me to do.

"What's now been so important to me is seein' what happens to people. After you've shined a place up, people say, 'Now this is really pretty!' And you'd say, 'Thanks.' But the important thing is that if he or she recognized it, there's a peace there for them. They'll say, 'This is pretty,' and then sit down and pray in a way they couldn't if they sat down and said, 'Boy, this place is really filthy.' I really see the results in people bein' able to worship. It helps give them a peace. What I do points them further to the Lord.

"I remember the scriptures talkin' about Jesus preparin' a place for us in heaven. I see myself preparin' a place for worship and a place that is better to live in. Yeah, the word *work* means doin' what you have to do, but for me it's prayin' itself. And when you go in to clean a floor and polish it and walk out and see it shine, that's the answer to the cleanin'. Like the *Constitution* sez, 'I'm to do it with joy.' I do, because what I do can cause somethin' to happen to people."

During the year of ongoing study and the disciplines of community life came three evaluations by the community and Father John about how the novices were doing. In Jim's case, at the conclusion of his year as a novice, he was recommended to take temporary vows. A Mass was celebrated during which Jim took vows covering a three-year period, which was his preparation for final vows of a lifelong commitment as a brother. This three-year period was a time in which Jim was to ask, "Lord, is this really where you want me to be?" During this period the community also was asking if this was where Jim was to be.

With his year as a novice at an end and his temporary vows taken, Jim was assigned to Saint Fidelis Seminary High School in Herman, Pennsylvania, a boarding school for boys, with Father Lester Knoll as its principal. Jim was brought there as Director of Maintenance and Student Work Supervisor. In addition to these tasks, he continued his study and the carrying out of his temporary vows under the supervision of Father Lester, who was also his spiritual director.

The day before Brother Jim's arrival at Saint Fidelis, an assembly was called. No one knew why, and the noisy hall was filled with student conversations about possible reasons for it. Soon the principal, Father Lester, arrived and the noise stopped. As he began to speak, nothing had prepared the students for what they were about to hear. They were told, "Brother Jim Townsend is coming to be Director of

Maintenance and Student Work Supervisor for the school, overseeing all of your work assignments. Now you also need to know that Brother Jim is an ex-convict who, prior to coming here, just finished his novice training at Saint Conrad's Friary in Annapolis, Maryland."

All coughing and fidgeting and rustling of papers stopped at the word *ex-convict*. Everyone was at complete attention. Father Lester went on to tell them that Jim had committed murder and had served twenty years in prison. "It is important," said Father Lester, "that you know the story and that you welcome him as he will be supervising your work. I believe that as you come to know Brother Jim you all will like him."

Jim's arrival was met with apprehension among many students, but nothing to equal the anxiety Jim was feeling. *Lord, I am so uncomfortable. I'm scared. I feel like I don't have any know-how to work with these kids. I feel like everyone is lookin' at me and wonderin' about me. I wish right now that I could deal with what they're thinkin'. They don't know it yet, but they got more learnin' than I do. This is gonna take time.*

Getting involved with the students occurred instantly, however, as Jim had to hand out their work assignments. But it took some time before the students began to feel comfortable with him. As Jim increasingly was called upon to show the kids how to do cleaning and maintenance work, they began to grow in self-confidence and to trust him.

One day the mother of one of the kids asked her son how he was getting along without her. He said, "Don't worry, Mom. I got another mother. His name is Brother Jim!" Another student introduced Jim to his mother who was visiting on campus. He said, "Brother Jim, I want you to meet my mom." "Oh," she said, "I've been wanting to meet you because our neighbors are jealous. My windows really shine. He's learned a lot!" Jim said, "I had to punish him one day by doin' extra time on windows, so I had him up on the ladder doin' those." He pointed up to the third floor. "You had my son up there?" she asked. Jim said, "Yeah, and I can assure you I was holdin' the ladder."

In a meeting one day with Father Lester, as he was reviewing the work detail, Jim pointed out, "Gettin' ninth graders started is somethin'. They really don't know what the heck is goin' on when it comes to doin' any kind of cleanin'. I told this one kid, 'You run down to the kitchen and tell the lady you want a corn broom.' He shot off down the hallway and stopped dead, turned around, ran back, and asked, 'What is a corn broom?' When he brought it up, he asked, 'Is this made out of corn?' Well, then I actually had to teach him how to use a broom. His mom, of course, did all that stuff. When these kids sweep, the dust would choke the life out of you. I'd have to tell 'em, 'No, no, no—you just drag it along the ground.'

"Ya know, Father, we've got some smokers in the ranks, sneakin' around, even though they know smokin' is not allowed. Smokin' is bad for you. I know that from all the smokin' I did years ago. We've got this one kid who smokes like a chimney. I'd confront him about it and he says, 'Yeah, yeah.' But one day I was up in the tower, and I was lookin' around thinkin' what a great view this is, and I spotted this kid. I could tell the way he was messin' around that he had somethin' going on down there. Then I saw smoke. Then he started messin' around where this one tree was. *Now what's this all about,* I sez to myself. So I went down to where he had been and started lookin' around. A half hour later I found it—his stash of cigarettes. It was in one of them holes a squirrel makes in a tree. A half carton of butts. I took 'em and I didn't say nothin' to him. Later I could tell by the way he was actin' that he was upset. I finally got him aside and laid them on the table and sez, 'You're not gonna get ahead of me, man. You'd better stop this stuff. It's gonna kill you, for cryin' out loud.' He looked at me and said, 'How did you find them?' I sez, 'I have my ways.'

"Then there was another incident with this same kid. We was all on a school bus on our way to a sporting event. I was one of the supervisors. I was sittin' up in the front of the bus and he was smokin' in the back. He's figurin', 'The big dummy up there can't see me.' He held his hand out the window. So when he was getting' off the bus I said, 'Now I'll take them cigarettes.' He looks at me and sez, 'How'd you know?' And I sez, pointing, 'That's what rearview mirrors is for!'

"Father, in workin' with these guys, I think I'm able to show them how to do a lot of things and enable them to learn and grow and be responsible. This is really great to see. In these work assignments I have some kids doin' bathrooms, others do floors, classrooms, and outside work as well. But ya know, more often now, all of a sudden while we're workin' a kid will say, 'Can we talk about this or that?' So while workin' or stoppin' for a bit, we'd talk."

"What are some of the things you talk about?" asked Father Lester.

"Well, one of the things we talk about a lot are parents and, in a lot of cases, moms who want their sons to become priests. Yeah, this kid sez to me one day, 'I'm not too sure about all this, Brother Jim. I don't want to hurt nobody, but I'm not wantin' to become a brother or a priest.'"

"What did you say to him?" Father asked.

"I said, 'Bein' a brother or a priest is a way of life. You don't do it to please your mom. This may be your mom's vocation for you, but if it's not yours, then it's not right. You should talk with Father Lester. You might have to say to your mom, 'It's not for me.' She'll get over it; otherwise you'll do yourself and everyone else a lot of harm. Don't lie to yourself.' This kid shared his goal of becomin' a chiropractor. I bet he'll make it."

"What else are you talking about with the kids?" Father Lester asked.

"Stuff like their feelins about their studies, sex, fears—you name it. I'm learnin' that kids really talk when they're ready. I'm discoverin' I can't plan it. I'm to be ready when they are or I might lose the chance.

"One day a kid wanted to talk and he said he wasn't too sure if the Lord would really listen to him. He was talkin' about wantin' an answer to a particular prayer. 'Yeah, Brother Jim, I just don't have that feeling that he would listen.' I sez, 'I think what you're sayin' is, 'Lord, here's what I need right now—and hurry up! Right?' 'Well, yeah,' he said. I answered, 'He doesn't do it that way. Listen, you just turn yourself over to the Lord and tell him that by yourself (and that's the big thing) you're not gonna make it. Just be at peace and in his time and in his way things will evolve. Don't ever say to him, 'Here's what I want right now.' Just say, 'Lord, this is what I'm thinkin'. What do you think?' And then put it in his hands."

"Jim, with what you've been experiencing thus far in working with these kids, what do you want to happen?" Father asked.

"Lookin' at my rotten past," Jim responded, "I just want these guys to grow and learn to become good men, husbands, fathers, brothers, priests, whatever. This is what Father Walsh at Rockview and the older priests and brothers at Saint Conrad's wanted for me. This awareness has a lot to do with some new, deep stuff goin' on in my life. I'm really finally seein' something—that what I did, and do now, affects other people. We know my education's not much. I haven't written a book or anything and I'm not famous or known by many. I'm not a bishop or the pope and never will be, but I need to be present with and hear the experiences of the older priests and brothers and those I look to for guidance. I have accepted that what I did at Rockview and with the others I've been tryin' to help since, that I mean somethin' to other people.

"There is a word I've discovered that wasn't part of my past growin' up. The word is *significant*. I had to look it up to discover that it means 'havin' meaning and importance.' What has become a totally new thought for me is that I am significant and have significance in the world. The Lord did it all. Imagine me, Jimmy Townsend, significant!"

After two years at Saint Fidelis, Jim was transferred back to Saint Conrad's Friary in Annapolis. A new guardian had arrived, Father Scott Seethaler, the new Director of Novices, and it was important that someone who knew the details of maintenance and who could establish and manage work assignments be there to give support and ease Father Scott's responsibilities as he got started.

"Father Scott," Jim said, "one day, a novice says to me, 'Brother Jim, you always want to paint. Can we talk about this job?' The novice was looking up at the second floor at the large window and its frame that had to be painted. He looked afraid.' So I said to him, 'No problem. You just paint the inside of the frame and the room, and I will climb the ladder and do the outside.'

"I tell you this story because doin' what I'm doin' with the novices gives me a great opportunity to start relationships with them and maybe be of help. You know it wasn't too long before this guy and I were talkin' about important stuff. I know we'll become friends. The novices are beginnin' to know that if they want to talk, my door is always open."

"Jim," asked Father Scott, "What do you say to them when they come to you for help?"

"I tell 'em what I think, or I suggest that they talk with a particular priest, or I let 'em know I'm just available to listen while they talk about their feelings or tough personal or theological struggles. Best of all, though, is when we pray together. Father, I'm thinkin' that one of the most important things I can communicate is that I'm not perfect like some stained-glass saint up in a window. Ya know, with all the hurt I've caused, the most difficult thing I had to face was the truth of all my flaws and frailties. But it was in seein' the truth about myself, and growin' with a sense of forgiveness, that I'm knowin' more and more that God loves me just like I am. Some of these guys don't feel good about themselves for whatever reason, and I'm hopin' that in me not bein' perfect but feelin' loved anyway that maybe they'll have some good thoughts about themselves."

"Jim, there are some other people I want you to talk to and be available to also," said Father Scott. "I'm continually concerned about the kids in our high school. One of the ways I handle my concern is to provide a weekly assembly, exposing the students to speakers in whose lives God has powerfully moved. I want you to speak to this weekly gathering. I know your story and you certainly would give them a lot to think about."

"Well, Father, do you usually make an announcement about coming speakers? What would you say about me?"

"I would state that we are going to have someone with us next week who met with a lot of difficulty in his life, but who wound up doing pretty well. Sometimes I refer to Saint

Paul who was knocked off his horse and had to deal with God's plan for his life and how God helped him on his way. I won't tell them any more. I just want you to get up and tell your story."

Jim did that a week later, and Father Scott commented, "The questions these kids asked were good ones. I hope you realize they really listened to you. You have to know that the Lord used you powerfully." Jim reflected, *Lord, this story never seems to get stale for others. How do you do that?*

As well as being part of the growth process of the novices, Jim continued to work on his own spiritual growth as he lived out his temporary vows. Periodic evaluations of his progress took place and eventually he attended a six-day retreat that focused on his preparation for his taking final vows. Then, on February 9, 1976, Jim was brought back to St. Augustine's Church in the Lawrenceville section of Pittsburgh. At a special Mass attended by the priests and brothers of the province and the Pittsburgh Diocese, Jim made his life commitment. Upon his return to Maryland he received a phone call that he immediately shared with his supervisor. "Father, I was just told that I am no longer on parole!"

"What a moment this must be for you, Jim," responded Father Scott. "Congratulations. This has taken a long time."

"Father, you know there are so many new things happenin' to me. I just became a brother and I know that this is what God wants me to be doin'. But this phone call tells me that the Lord just brought to an end the old—the last legal chain to my past and all the hurt I did to cause it. I can't wait to get the official letter because it will serve as a reminder of the changes God has made in my life. I was just thinkin' and laughin' on my way over here. I was rememberin' when I accepted the Lord at Rockview and it didn't matter to me whether or not I got released. I had everythin' I needed, including work and ministry. I really believed that that was where I could best serve the Lord. I was free before I got out of prison. But today I have a new freedom, kinda like I'm fully released into the world with no more chains."

The next morning Jim told Father Scott, "After last night, enjoyin' the apple pie the cook made for my celebration, I went to the chapel and just sat down and said, 'Yo, Lord.' I just sat there in peace and freedom, like there was nothin' to hold me back anymore. Sittin' there I realized, like Paul says in Second Corinthians 5:17, 'If anyone is in Christ, he is a new creation, the old has passed away, behold the new has come.' The old had passed away. It was finished. I fell asleep."

CHAPTER 11

Cleveland

"Because of Cleveland I have come to realize that the American society that locked me up was now trustin' me and lettin' me know that I was of value to them." Jim made this statement to Father Gary, his guardian, and the other priests and brothers at Saint Paul's Friary in Cleveland as he was about to conclude his ministry there. Thirteen years earlier, the Province in which Jim was a brother took on a new commitment to provide a pastor for Saint Paul's Shrine and a chaplain to the Poor Clare Nuns in a convent next to the friary. It was the spring of 1976 when Jim was asked if he would leave Saint Conrad's in Maryland and go to Saint Paul's Friary in Cleveland as Director of Maintenance for both the friary and the convent. Upon becoming a new brother and ending his parole, Jim felt an increased sense of adventure in his newfound freedom. He said yes.

When the van pulled up in front of the friary, Jim felt an immediate anxiety as he looked out the window of the van and across the street. Jim had never forgotten what a hooker looked like and there they were, with their pimps, hanging out on the street corner. For the first ten days he was in an internal battle and struggle with temptation. By the tenth day, he knew that he was in serious trouble and the direction seemed very clear: *Hey, Jimmy! This ain't for you here. Get yourself now to Father Gary. Get out of here while you can.*

When he arrived at Father Gary's office to tell him, "I'm out of here," Father Gary said, "Jim, will you please put this new license plate on the car? I have to use it in an hour."

As Jim pulled the paper off the license plate on his way to the car, he was astounded by what he saw, and he knew instantly that he was to stay at Saint Paul's. Upon his return to Father Gary, he laughed, "Ya know, when I pulled the paper off of that plate I was blown away. I, who knew all about license plates, having made thousands of them in prison, saw God givin' me a message through this one. So help me, Father, the message was instant.

"Ya know, Father, if ten days ago I had just gone to the chapel and said 'Lord, I'm upset here. I'm scared. You know I want those girls! If I had done that, I could have started to work it through, but no, not me. I have to be in charge. When you told me to put that license plate on the car, I was comin' to tell you I had to leave Saint Paul's because the temptation was too much for me with these prostitutes so available. But then I looked at the license plate. It is red and white, has four holes so it can be bolted to the car, and reads *L530473P*. I swear, Father, it spoke to me as if I was readin' it off a piece of paper."

Father Gary waited. Then Jim continued, "The L stands for my life sentence. 530 was my prison number, and 47 was when I started my sentence. Your time starts when you're arrested. When you add up these numbers—53047—they total 19, which was my age when I was arrested in 1947. I was thinking about the 3P so I went back over the plate again, and what came to me was that the L also stands for love. I sorta like the L because it's like a rockin' chair. The Lord sits in it and he'll rock you back and forth until you feel good again. The 5 stands for the Lord's five wounds that he took just for me. The 3 is the Holy Trinity: Father, Son, and Holy Spirit. The 0 stands for family—you know, there's no end. The 4 is for the four Gospels. Saint Francis said, 'Just read the four Gospels. It's all right there.' The 7 is the big number. You do it seven days a week, not now and then. Like you say, 'Lord, I've got this problem.' Then maybe six months later you say, 'Lord, I've got another problem.' But you don't stay close enough to say, 'Thanks.' The 3 stood for my third assignment since bein' a brother, and with the P I seemed to hear, 'Park and be at peace.' In other words, 'Jimmy, where I put you, you'll grow and you'll grow when you accept my graces and use them. The four holes mean that he's at the four corners of the earth. He's always been there and always will be."

Cleveland brought into Jim's life a never-ending stream of new challenges, new people, and new teachings. One day at the cathedral, he told the story of the license plate and a lady from another church came to him and said, "Can I have your autograph?"

"What for?" Jim asked.

"I want your permission to use it, and the things you said in your talk. The people in my church need to hear things like this so they can become more aware of the ways God might be trying to speak to them in their own lives."

"Use it any way you want, and thanks. Ya know, I'm just thinkin' that this license plate experience happened so I will not in the future limit the ways God's tryin' to make himself heard. He needs me to be available to him so through me he can speak to others like you."

It wasn't long before he received more invitations to speak. One was at a very large annual Christian conference that centered on prayer and the gifts of the Holy Spirit for ministry—prophecy, discernment, speaking in tongues, and so on. Jim was asked to speak on the Lord's transforming power in his life. When he was finished, the next speaker was a woman who had been badly crippled and in constant pain. In her presentation she stated that she told the Lord that she would go and witness to his power if he would take away the pain and enable her to walk with crutches. She was standing there because the Lord did just that.

In the midst of her talk, the woman sitting next to Jim, who was moved by what she was hearing and convicted that the Lord wanted her to use the gifts she had been given, leaned over to Jim and said, "I have a message for you."

"Oh?" Jim responded.

She said, "I didn't know that you had been married. I'm to tell you that your son is waiting for you." *What's this?* Jim thought. *It's been a long time since my nightmares stopped, with Alice and a young child appearin' before me every night, both lookin' so sad. I think of Alice every day, but I never knew prior to this that the child would have been a son. I wonder what happened to Bill who was with me at Rockview. I remember thinkin' that I could have had a son who would be like him. Wow, what would his name be? Lord, this makes that little child in the nightmares more real. Thank you that you helped me know I was forgiven before this. It still hurts to know that I killed him. Oh Jesus.*

One day as Jim was coming into the friary office, Mary Ann, the secretary, stopped him and said, "Who is Ida? She certainly knows you and talks like you two are good friends."

"We are," Jim responded. "I first met her when she was eighty-nine years old and I'll never forget her. She is a black lady and she was always havin' to go to the doctor so I began to take her to her appointments. Then I started helpin' her with her shoppin'. I'd pick her up at the doctor's office or wherever and she'd say, 'Is my grandmother here?'

Everyone would say, 'Her what?' We had a lot of fun. One day she taught me a great lesson in humility and bein' at peace with yourself.

"This one day she sez, 'Would you like to see my husband's grave? He was a veteran who died in '46 right after the war was over.' We got to the graveyard and she sez, 'Drive down 'till you see three bushes.' We got out of the car and found the gravesite. As we headed toward it, there were two elderly white women and one said, 'The only thing wrong with this cemetery is that nigger they put in here.' I'm thinkin', 'Oh, no. What now?' But my friend walked over to the white woman and said, 'Don't worry. If he gets a look at you, he'll get up and walk to another place.'

"I went over to her and said, 'That was great. I couldn't have done better.' But what got to me was that then she said, 'I learned a long time ago that I am who I am and I better be true to that. That's the way God's gonna judge me.' What a lesson for Jim Townsend! Ida and me, we talk about a lot of different things and pray about different things. I even do her bankin'. She writes a note to the bank and I cash her checks and bring the money to her. She is a beautiful, kind, and gentle woman. I always call her 'Grandma' 'cause that's who she is to me. I love bein' with her. I couldn't have a better relationship with my real grandmother.

"In my final days in prison I was aware that the guys of the Third Order and Father Walsh had really begun to trust me. Ida, however, trusts me with her whole life and with the important stuff of her day. I break up when I think of it. What has become so clear, finally, is that you can't have a relationship without trustin'. I've had to work hard to earn this trust. The Lord sent Ida to me and I'm so grateful for her."

One day Jim was in the office and said, "Ya know, Mary Ann, I am wonderin' at times whether I'm in

Cleveland so that the Lord can use me in some way for other people, or whether I'm here so that the Lord can use circumstances and other people to change or challenge me."

"It's both, Jim," she replied.

One night Jim learned that you never say no to God and that none of our life experiences is wasted. He uses them all. Jim was returning to the friary with Jake, a postulant who was studying at Saint Paul's to be a brother. They had come to the front steps of the church next to the friary when they saw a hooker waiting for a customer. Jim was reminded of his arrival in Cleveland several years earlier and being overwhelmed with temptation as he saw the hookers gathered across the street. Jake told Jim to wait behind, but within earshot of his conversation with this heavily made-up teenage girl.

"Did you ever think about getting out of this?" Jake asked, as she began to give him a list of prices for different sexual acts. She responded with, "Are you a cop?" He said, "No, but we can help you if you'll let us. I know a place where you can go and rest awhile. Then we can talk about things, like if you have relatives or a place to go." She walked away.

When Jake returned, Jim said, "You know, Jake, you're good at this. How do you know so much?"

"I started doing this in DC," Jake replied. "But you know, you have to be careful. You could get your head bashed in by the pimps."

Watching this interaction between Jake and the hooker, Jim saw a demonstration of compassion and concern on Jake's part that was at the risk of personal harm to him. It was clear that his need to be there for her was greater than the consequences that could befall him. Jim, who had risked and fought his whole life, felt a compelling call to go and do likewise. *Lord, you're something else! The temptation I had to work through when I first got to Cleveland seein' them girls was gettin' me ready for now, wasn't it? You're somethin' else!*

After that night Jim began a ministry to prostitutes that continued through the balance of his seven years in Cleveland. Father Gary, who continually consulted with him about this ministry, was stunned one morning when Jim showed up with bruises on his face and arms. "I guess it's not hard to see I got beat up, but I think she heard some things I said," Jim said.

"What happened?" asked Father Gary.

"Well, it's like I usually do. I go to a place and a girl comes up to me and asks me if I want a good time. I say, 'Yeah, but what I really want is to see you do better for yourself.' I usually make suggestions and sometimes we talk and sometimes I am told to drop dead. Last night I said, 'I just want you to know that there is a better way if you want it, and there is a chance to get out of your prison,' but a pimp surprised me before I could go any further."

Another morning when Jim and Father Gary were meeting, Father asked, "Jim, you told me that our secretary, Mary Ann, asked you to take her to the special seminar on prostitution in Cleveland. How did that go?"

"Well, we went. You know, she didn't want to go by herself and I didn't blame her. I had my suit and collar on. We were drivin' there and I stopped for a red light. This girl came over and says, 'Hey, Father. Oh, I didn't see your bitch, Father.' She left, laughing. I looked at Mary Ann and said, 'Remember that!'

"So we got to the school where the talk was bein' given. This priest was seekin' funds to start a refuge for prostitutes on a farm in Lima, Ohio. Literally, a couple of guys would go out in a car and drive around and pick up some girls. They'd drive them somewhere, identify themselves, and say, 'Did you ever think of gettin' out of this? We have this place where you can get some rest, good food, a bath. Maybe you could finish school.' They had pretty good success with this place.

"But anyway, we're at this meetin' and I'm sittin' there mindin' my own business. I'm lookin' around and there's this one girl—she's about thirty years old, white, well-dressed, a do-gooder type. She looked like one of those persons that never had a hungry day in her life. So when the questions started, she suddenly stood up and said, 'I'm tired of hearing you people talking about getting money. If you need money, why don't you just say that you need ten thousand dollars to run this place and you need all the help you can get. Listen, there's no such thing as a ten- or eleven-year-old prostitute, boy or girl.'

"Well, Father, I'm sittin' there and finally I knew I had to get up. So I raised my hand, at the same time saying to Mary Ann, 'Forgive me for what I'm about to do,' and while I'm gettin' up, this do-gooder says to me, 'Oh come on, Father, you probably never got sexually excited in your life.' I said, 'Listen here, I had broads like you for breakfast before you were born!' This big heavy lady was sittin' next to me and said, 'Say, what?'

"Then I said, 'Can I have the floor for a couple of minutes?' I went up and told my story and said, 'The kind of work this guy is doin' ain't somethin' you publish in the newspaper. As I was given a chance, these boys and girls need a chance.' This woman then says to me, 'As long as you're confident in yourself, no one can hurt you.' I said, 'Is that right?' So I walked up and said, 'Let's assume that you're walking on an isolated street and a man comes up and attempts to rape you. What would you do?'

"In way of demonstration she started to kick, and I twisted her arm behind her back in such a way that she was in pain. I said, 'Now all I gotta do is whatever I want.' I let her go." At this point, Father Gary's jaw dropped in astonishment.

"'Now folks,' I told 'em," Jim continued. "'There are some situations where a person can back out. But there are many conditions where a person won't back out if they don't have any help because they've been beaten so bad and they're on dope and stuff like that. They're ruined. As far as they're concerned, they're not humans anymore. People have to back them up. So, Father, this girl was gettin' to me. I sez to myself, *She's the kind that can really be helped and be a help once she gets it.* We walked outside together and I said, 'See that guy over there? He's doin' off-duty work. That's how he makes extra money. I'm gonna ask him to drive us a couple of places and I'll show you what I mean.' She and her friend got in the car with Mary Ann and me and I sez, 'Take us up north where the cathedral is.' This was the major hangout. When we got up there, I pointed, 'See that girl over there? How old do you think she is?' She said, 'Thirteen or fourteen.' So I said, 'Watch what happens.'

"I got out of the car and walked over and asked, 'How ya doin', baby?' She sez, 'Hey, Father, half-price. I'll show you a good time for twenty bucks.' The women in the car heard this. So I sez, 'No, hon, I don't want that.' I had money, which I put in her hand, but I had another twenty bucks that I slipped into her dress. 'Do what you want with it,' I said. 'You might want to get on a bus and go somewhere.' 'Thanks, Father,' she said.

"Then I got in the car and asked, 'What did you think of that?' She said, 'I had to see it to believe it.' I told her that the off-duty officer with us could tell her that many of them are even younger than that girl was.

"Father, those who run this place are very protective of the kids and the program. They don't give out names or telephone numbers. I have never gone to the place where they bring the kids, but of course I know the ways to make a connection with a kid. As you know, Father, the police come to me from time to time with somebody and say, 'See what you can do here. You better take this opportunity.'

"This ministry sends kids out of state to relatives or somewhere to finish school or just to go off for ten days to get a rest and think. One girl who went there told me she washed her hair ten times before she felt clean. If someone is on dope, they have a way to ease them off it. They've had a 40–50 percent success rate. Yeah, there are those that run off, but this group of people never gives up on them. Like those I eventually met who never gave up on me. I never say no to any request to give a talk or fund raise."

Months later at a morning meeting with Father Gary, Jim said, "Father, you need to know what came out of that night with the young do-gooder type lady who was such a pain. She has become one of the best friends this ministry ever had. She has given a lot of money but she also does a lot of work like cookin' and cleanin'. Because of people like this lady, this ministry is still goin' on. This is probably one of the best experiences I've had in Cleveland." After a period of silence Father Gary asked, "Jim, what have all these years in Cleveland meant to you?"

Jim thought a moment, then said, "I was thinkin' that when I was at Saint Fidelis I realized I had meaning for others. They, for whatever reason, said I was important to them and I came to believe that I was significant. But here in Cleveland, what with workin' with the police and other organizations, I've realized that I have gifts and stuff that they wanted to use. I've further realized that society was trustin' me and that I was of value to them. But I guess most important to me is that I am a part of God's plan for someone else and that this will keep happenin' when I stay open to receive it.

"Imagine wakin' up in the morning knowin' that you are worth somethin' just as you are. Imagine!"

Chapter 12

Being and Doing

"I'm sorry to tell you this but we've reviewed all the X-rays and have determined that you have colon cancer. It's serious."

This was the response of one of the doctors of the medical team Jim had visited some weeks earlier. The doctor went on to state, "Usually with this kind of cancer, death is within three years. Let me show you these X-rays and describe the surgery we're going to do." *Lord, what's gonna happen now?* Jim wondered. *How did all this happen? This is an enemy I don't know how to fight like I know how to fight some guy in the prison yard. I'm scared.*

A few months prior to this diagnosis, Jim had been given a new assignment, leaving Cleveland for Saint Conrad's Friary in Pittsburgh. He was needed once again to do the maintenance and to oversee the work schedules of the novices. Jim, as he had done in the past, used his position to establish a trust level with these young men. Many of them came to Jim with their problems and he was always available to listen to them.

It wasn't long after Jim's arrival in Pittsburgh that knowledge of his background traveled around the city, and he received speaking invitations from civic organizations and churches, both Catholic and Protestant. Fulfilling these engagements, plus conducting his annual mission to Rockview, he began to notice that the great energy he had always known was leaving him. As he thought about it, he realized that he had begun to feel a sense of fatigue during his last few months in Cleveland. He dismissed the symptoms he was experiencing as a hemorrhoid problem, which he treated with over-the-counter medications. When the pain, bleeding, and exhaustion increased, he finally became concerned, but went to the doctor only after his legs gave out from under him one night. After extensive tests he returned to the doctor's office for the diagnosis.

"How are you feeling about this?" asked the doctor.

"Well," Jim began. "I figure you know what's best so I'm goin' along with it. I know the Lord is here and I know that I need to accept the facts as they come about. It's gonna be humblin' to be worked over and cut open and to learn to deal with the colostomy. I know that if I don't go along with it, it's the end, so I'll give it a try."

Prior to the surgery a lot of his fear turned into thanksgiving that surgical methods were available and that God had put into the minds of his doctors the knowledge and ability to do such treatment. The surgery resulted in a sixteen-day hospital stay and an irreversible colostomy that, during his recuperation, made sleeping and dressing difficult. A new attitude and routine were forced onto what had been normal daily living. The colostomy bags had to be cleaned daily. All activity as he had known it came to an end for about seven months as his body demanded the rest and care necessary for healing and the regaining of his strength.

Day followed upon day, with an increasing awareness of the contrast between the inactivity forced upon him at this time with no predictable end and the years of demanding ministry filled with excitement and adventure. Through the years, since his awareness of the reality of Jesus in his life, "being" with the Lord and "doing" ministry, first in prison and then as a brother, became synonymous. With days of recuperation stretching into months, a new understanding of this period in his life and its purpose evolved. Jim no longer could be "doing" ministry as he had known it. What was he to do now?

Daily novices, priests, and brothers visited his room at the friary. Prayer was an essential part of each visit. When he was alone, he found flowing from deep within praise and thanksgiving for all the ways in which Gold had blessed him through the illness and for bringing him to this place of deep gratitude. He also saw this time as an opportunity just to be with the Lord in quiet contemplation. *That's what's happenin' isn't it, Lord? You're givin' me all this time to read and study and pray, but mainly to just be with you.*

One day in a visit, Brother Bob Herrick said, "Jim, during the many hours each day that you are alone up here, what's really going on? What do you do?"

"It's a time of just bein'," Jim answered. "It's in the quiet of sittin' here and bein' with the Lord that words just come to the surface. Things like, 'Oh, Jesus, I love you....I praise you....I'm so grateful....Let's talk about so and so I'm concerned about....Let me tell you the direction I need.' Stuff like that.

"Bob, what this cancer has done is to bring me to know in my heart that more than all the things I've been doin' in ministry, and the excitement in makin' a difference in someone else's life, that what I want more than anythin' is just to be with him. I know this! What I've been hearin' through all these days is 'Jimmy, you can't do the stuff I have in mind without first bein' with me to get the power to do it.' Bob, I'm not sayin' he hasn't been with me and done unbelievable stuff for me and in me, but what's different is that it's not just him doin' for me, but of me consciously bein' with him. It's a relationship with me bein' present with him as he is with me. Bob, I think he's been waitin' a long time for me to be able to come to this. I was readin' in Saint Mark the other day the passage where—remember when Jesus had sent out the disciples in a mission to teach all, and then they came back, and Jesus didn't ask them to all report in and let's have a meetin'. No, he sez, 'Come be with me.' You guys can't keep goin' out and doin' stuff without getting' rest and power.'

"Bob, I know that the Lord didn't cause the cancer in me, but he sure used it so I know what has to come first."

Jim's full recovery took two years. Then he heard that he was to go to Washington, DC, to be in charge of maintenance at Capuchin College, a Capuchin Friary focused on the formation of the young friars after they have taken their first vows. When he heard of his new assignment, he thought:

Lord, you've had me all to yourself for the last two years as I have been healin'. There is a quiet inside I've never known before. You took me out of the world I'd been in and brought me to a place where you could speak to me and where all the demands and noise of my daily life was taken away so I could hear what you're thinkin' that's most important for me. Oh, Lord, will I ever have a time like this again? You have built into my guts a memory of our relationship of closeness that I'll never forget. I don't want to leave here and be sent back into the world, but maybe you're sendin' me back because you got my priorities straight. Now I think I am ready to do your work again 'cause you and I know that what I'll do will come out of first bein' together.

Soon after his arrival in Washington, some friends invited Jim to speak at a very large Protestant conference held on the Eastern Shore of Maryland. A man had a big piece of property and made it available to a large diverse group of Christians each year. Jim was one of several speakers invited. After he finished speaking one day, he met a minister who looked, as Jim put it, "down in the dumps." The minister told Jim, "Man, I've got a problem. I've got four places I have to go and I can't even be at two of those places at the same time. I've got to get people here and then go there and then come back here."

"Let me pick up the people for you," Jim suggested. "Would you mind?" said the minister. "No problem," Jim answered. Jim was wearing his brown Franciscan habit behind the wheel of the bus as he drove six miles to the church where he was to pick up his passengers. Then he got out and stood beside the bus. As the people came out of the church, they heard him say, "All right, all of you Protestants, get in the bus. Let's go!"

The minister of the church came up to Jim and asked, "Well, who are you?" A lady who had heard Jim speak at the church said, "Oh, Pastor, don't miss him. He's a nut. He's a Capuchin." At the same time another woman came up to the minister and whispered in his ear, with which the minister turned to Jim and said, "I hear you have a story to tell about your life. The minister who is supposed to preach tomorrow is sick. Would you mind reading the Gospel and telling your story?"

Jim replied, "I'm not all that good at readin' out loud, but I'll do it."

The minister asked, "How should I introduce you?"

"Aw, just tell 'em I'm a Capuchin brother you found in front of the church."

The minister said, "After you talk, the second collection is yours." The next day after the service ended, Jim and the minister stood in amazement as the money in the collection plate was counted. "Jim, there is $340.00 here. No one has ever gotten this much before."

Jim put the envelope of cash on Father Superior Joe Mindling's desk back at Capuchin College on Monday morning. Father finished counting it and turned to Jim saying, "Don't you ever, ever turn down any of these invitations to speak!" He never did. As in other cities where Jim had served, word of mouth from people who had heard Jim brought other invitations to speak in churches and prisons. Washington was no exception.

Alex, one of the college students who had gotten to know Jim, asked, "Brother Jim, after all you went through in prison all those years, why do you go back?"

"Alex, ever since I got out of Rockview, I've gone back for the weekend that includes Saint Dismas Day. Remember that Dismas was the one on the cross next to Jesus who asked him for mercy. I go back to give back, to be there for the inmates, and to tell the story of what happened to me. I want them to know about God's power to change a life, and I hope someone might find somethin' to gain hope and new direction for his life. I've found that when I go to be with them they really listen to me because they know I've walked in their shoes and they know that I know what I'm talkin' about. What keeps blowin' me away is that God uses the most awful and unforgivable parts of my story and turns them into something good for someone else. As you prepare yourself for the priesthood, you need to think about your own life as you're learning about who God is.

"What happened this last time at Rockview, Alex, was that the warden came to me at the conclusion of the weekend and said, 'Jim, you know that leading up to this weekend every year is a week-long spiritual mission culminating on Saint Dismas Day. I think that beginnin' next year you should come for the whole week, speak at different times durin' the week, and have more individual time with the inmates.' Alex, what a gift this is for me. They see that much change that they have confidence I'm OK. Like what happened to me in Cleveland, I'm again realizin' I was put in prison by our society but because of the change in me this same prison is asking me to come back and help."

Jim asked, "Alex, are you hearin' anything out of what I'm sayin' for your own life?"

"Yeah," Alex said, "I'm hearing that God doesn't waste anything from our life experiences. He uses it for us and for others who all of a sudden hear something for themselves. Jim, going back to the prison has got to tell you that your past hasn't been a total loss. I won't forget this in my own dark future times of failure."

"We know, Alex, what also isn't a total loss is that I'm findin' a whole new ministry bein' given to me. I'm meetin' cancer patients all the time. Suddenly we have a lot to talk about!"

"Brother Jim, I hope someday I can see my life as having worth or meaning for someone else. You know, your guardian, Father Joe, and I were talking about this and we were talking about you in this regard," Alex said.

"What about me?" Jim asked.

"Well, I think you'll have to ask him."

Several days later as Jim was finishing a meeting with Father Joe concerning maintenance problems, he said, "Oh, by the way, I understand from Alex that you guys were talkin' about me the other day."

"That's true," Father Joe responded. "Jim, we have five young men in this community who will be preparing for the priesthood, but you know, one of the things I'm dealing with, either on an individual basis or in confession, is that not all of them feel good about themselves in one way or another. Your name comes up from time to time. Jim, the students, knowing about you, watch you as you work around here. They believe that you like what you do, and that you like yourself. But how can that be, they wonder? Isn't the work menial and boring? Isn't there something more significant you could see yourself doing, or want to do? Jim, what's your response to this thinking? I'd like to quote you."

"No," Jim answered. "I don't wish that I were doin' somethin' different or that I was more learned or athletic or handsome so I'd really have worth or self-esteem. Since my time in Rockview and findin' God's acceptance of me and love for me, I have come to a new place. No question, I used to feel bad about myself in a lot of different areas, but I feel good about my work. I take great satisfaction in doing it well. But you said somethin' a couple of months ago that took me to an even better place inside concernin' what I do and how I feel about myself.

"We had gathered for a meeting of the community and a time of prayer and you said, 'Boy, look at those floors. We've never seen them look like this before.'

"Father, in other places where I've worked in the past, people have said this too, but somethin' connected this time inside of me which is all new. When you said that the floors were great, there welled up in me a response that wasn't from my head, it came from out of my heart. 'I just love this work!' This was from the center of my gut—it was an 'aha.' Ya know what I'm sayin'? I was thinkin' at the moment when you said that about the floors that God gave me both the ability and the desire and the excitement to do this work. I didn't drum that up myself. Then I thought, 'This is who I am and it's all good. I'm not sittin' around wantin' to be someone other than me.' Several years ago I was ashamed and felt less about myself because I was a brother and not a priest. One night in prayer I heard somewhere inside, 'Jim, if I wanted you to be a priest, I would have made you one.' Father, I love bein' who I am and what I'm doin'. You can quote me. Gettin' to this place has come out of spendin' time alone with the Lord. I wouldn't know how to get to the place by myself."

CHAPTER 13

The Jim Townsend Award

Jim's car was traveling along the winding five-mile country road that led from Butler, Pennsylvania, northeast to Herman. Looking out the window, he noticed that not much had changed since the last time he had driven along this road except that some new homes dotted the landscape where previously there had been endless stretches of farmland.

Jim remembered traveling this same route in 1972 when, in the midst of his post-novitiate training, he was assigned to work at Saint Fidelis Seminary High School in Herman. He remembered the anxiety and fear he felt, wondering whether, as an ex-con, the students would accept him and whether he would be able to relate to the Saint Fidelis Community.

The winding road started gradually climbing. More houses appeared on each side of the road. Suddenly Jim saw the tower of the church ahead and then the fire hall immediately on his left just before the crossroad at the crest of the hill. After the intersection, as the road began a steep descent, the Saint Fidelis athletic field came into view. Next to it was a large green pond, disturbed by the heavy activity of Canada geese and several species of ducks. After a quick glimpse at that view, Jim turned his attention to the left, the scene of a significant part of his past and now his future. There stood the church of Saint Mary of the Assumption. From his point of view the church and its surrounding buildings could have been located in any number of little towns in

Italy as they dominated the horizon north, east, south, or west. The church's red brick façade was connected to the church house with a classic Romanesque arched portico. The tall arborvitae that lined the south wall of the church resembled the tall cypresses of Rome.

What a contrast the beauty of this is to the old scary-lookin', commanding Uniontown courthouse and jail where I sat in handcuffs and leg irons, Jim reflected. Just past the church was a driveway. It led through the church parking lot along the north end of the church house, between the larger complex of buildings of Saint Fidelis Seminary. Memories of his days in his first assignment as a Capuchin brother clamored for attention, but they quickly were put aside as the car stopped at an entrance at the end of Saint Mary's Hall. This was the Hermitage, his new home.

In 1989, while Jim was still at Capuchin College in Washington, DC, Father Lester phoned to remind him of a dream they had shared to start a Hermitage, a special Capuchin community with specific spiritual disciplines. The priests and brothers in this residence would spend fifty percent of their time in a contemplative life, participating in daily meditation, worship, and prayer, and fifty percent of their time in service and ministry to the world around them. The way had been cleared with the Pittsburgh Diocese for this residence to be established and Father Lester was appointed its first guardian or superior. Father Cyrus Gallagher and Jim would form the beginning community.

The Hermitage began at Holy Trinity Monastery in South Butler, a community north of Pittsburgh, in which the Byzantine Benedictines rented a house to them. For two years it served well as a place to begin this experiment. They, the hermits, were then given the opportunity to move behind the parish church of Saint Mary's of the Assumption in Herman.

With bag and baggage the cars headed north to Herman and finally pulled up at the entrance of the Hermitage.

Jim's daily responsibilities included the maintenance of the facility along with cooking and whatever else was necessary to make the community run smoothly. The immediate official ministry of the Hermitage was to the spiritual well-being of the residents of the Sunnyview Nursing Home. In addition to his work there and his continued ministry to prisoners, Jim served as a liaison between the Hermitage religious community, the village of Herman, the grade school, and the public. Whatever other ministries developed would flow out of the daily contemplative life of the Hermitage community.

Jim quickly discovered the grounds behind Saint Mary's and Saint Fidelis Seminary. They provided a magnificent view of the valley to the north and a perfect spot for quiet prayer and the inspiration of sunsets. Early one evening when the sunset inspired a great sense of God's presence, Jim began to review how God had led him in his life through all his assignments, from Saint Conrad's in Annapolis, where he began his novitiate training, to Capuchin College in DC, and then finally the drive into Herman. It now had been many years since the starting of the Hermitage, which had become a whole new adventure. Through his years in Herman he was having an experience unlike any since becoming a novice.

In the Hermitage in Herman, the small community of brothers and priests followed the Capuchin discipline of spending half their time in prayer and penance and half their time in ministry to the world and the needs around them. Herman was an ideal place for this to happen. Attached as it was to Saint Mary's Church, the Hermitage was on a major thoroughfare, the center of the Herman community. Jim's travels took him daily to the local grocery store, post office, gas stations, trade shops, and so on, where he would run into members of Saint Mary's and interact with others in the community. In other assignments he was seen as Brother Jim, the ex-con who had a great story of God's power and who could spellbind audiences. Now he was seen not so much as a phenomenon but as part of Herman's daily life, developing relationships with members of the community on many different levels.

One way to determine Jim's contact with his neighbors in Herman had to do with the particular food that ended up on the refectory table at mealtimes. Over the years he met every good cook in town and was never hesitant to make known his favorite meals. This was especially true regarding pastries. Two months before his birthday each year he "leaked" the information in the village and when the day arrived the sideboard in the refectory looked like the window of a bakery. One Herman lady continually stated, "Who can resist when he turns on that smile and that sense of humor, with those eyes that sparkle."

When Jim had to go into Butler for an appointment or on an errand, he never hesitated to call someone to drive him. Karen, a dear friend, stated in a letter to Father Lester, "It's always a small favor that he asks, but in return the advice and wisdom he shares make me a better person. I don't think he's ever going to know the tremendous impact he makes in this world. I know for certain that because of Jim I've come to love others as they are instead of trying to make them into what I perceive they should be. To love Jim and to know him leaves no choice but to accept and love others as Jesus does and Jim does."

Within walking distance of the Hermitage was a small grocery story, and Jim made many trips there to buy snacks for the kids in the parish grade school that he visited every-day. He was present for the faculty as well as the kids in the morning and sometimes at lunch or even at the end of the school day. He took little bags of snacks and slipped them to the kids in their classrooms or at recess, getting them all excited, and then leaving it to the teachers to get everyone settled down so that they could start to teach again.

On a particular report-card day Father Jim Kurtz, the pastor, and Sister Martha, the principal, had commitments that prevented them from reviewing the report cards with the kids. Brother Jim was asked to fill in for them. He was given specific instructions regarding the procedures for meet-ing with the students, reviewing their grades, and discussing where improvements were necessary. When each student came to him, however, he just stated, "You're doin' a great job, keep up the good work." There were many handshakes and hugs exchanged, followed later by a unanimous vote among the kids that they wanted Brother Jim to do report-card reviews in the future. He, however, was never invited to do it again.

Several weeks later, Jim had not been seen around the school for three days. The kids kept looking on and off at the classroom door expecting him to come at any time and sur-prise everyone with his great smile and sense of humor. It wasn't long before inquiries started, and Sister Martha, knowing that Jim was away on one of his prison missions, merely stated that Jim was in jail. All restlessness in the class-room ceased and the kids sat motionless, stunned expres-sions covering their faces. They didn't ask any more questions that day. After three days Brother Jim suddenly came through the door of the lunchroom, dressed in his brown robe and rope belt. The room erupted in spontaneous sustained cheers and the kids, leaving their lunch tables, surrounded him, making sure that he was OK. After keeping them in suspense as to why he was in jail, he finally told them that he had gone to the prison to help the inmates pray and deal with their problems.

Whoever knew Jim knew that his love for children came out of the deprivation in his childhood. He was determined that no child would leave his presence without knowing that he loved them and that God loved them. One of the visiting priests at the Hermitage stated, "Jim desires to be a light and hope to the children through the honor, the fun, and the joy of life. His transparency shows in his love of children."

In addition to its outreach into Herman and environs, the Hermitage also welcomed a continuous flow of visitors and developed an increasing reputation as a spiritual resource for retreats and spiritual direction. A priest who was on retreat at the Hermitage was visited one afternoon by a couple who were in their retirement years. Their children had long since left the nest, but their oldest daughter had been a source of concern for many years as she moved from one relationship to another. The situation was so bad that they disowned her when she told them that she was going to marry a Hispanic inmate in the prison in which she worked. He had one more year before he would be released from prison. This was the last straw for her parents and more than they could handle.

During their afternoon visit with the priest, they were introduced to Brother Jim who happened to be walking by the sitting room area, and when Jim left, the priest told them his story. During the months that followed, Jim's story seemed to be their daily inspiration. Finally one day the couple concluded that if God's grace was powerful enough to transform a convict into a Franciscan brother, they should give God and their daughter and son-in-law a chance. The family became reconciled.

On the occasion of the twenty-fifth anniversary of Jim's investiture as a Capuchin brother, he received a letter from Bob Toomy, a fellow brother. "I probably have never told you the extent to which you have influenced my life," the letter read. "I came up to the Hermitage on retreat and Father Lester was not there. You greeted me warmly and showed me to my room. That night you shared your story with me and with the others on retreat. At that time I was a basket case, filled with conflicting ominous emotions regarding my search and my possible future as a Capuchin brother. After hearing your story, Jim, I thought, 'What are these Capuchins all about? If they let people like him join then anyone can get in.'

"Jim, how wrong I was. As I got to know you during the month that followed, I changed my mind and thought, 'Now I'll never get in if all the applicants have to be as holy and fraternal as Jim.' You played havoc with my decision-making, but once I got to know you I knew in my heart that this was the kind of community I wanted to join."

Elaine Buzzinotte from Pittsburgh had just lost her father and knew that a time of retreat at the Hermitage was essential for her at that moment. She sat nervously at the table during the evening meal on a particular day of fasting for the brothers and priests and declined all the "extras" that were offered. She found her anxiety rising and her discomfort growing. She asked herself what she was doing there with such holy men. She couldn't wait to escape back to the safety and solitude of her little cabin and to be alone with her insecurities and inadequacies. Somehow, as the meal progressed, she began to feel more at ease. In her journal she wrote, "I realized that this 'ease' had to do with Brother Jim.

He is blessed with a natural sense of how to cut through it all in the most basic ways and make someone comfortable in the most stressful of circumstances.

"I'm still a little skittish about joining the community in communal prayer and meals. Today has been spent alone but this solitude just ended an hour ago as I heard 'Elaine… Elaine…Elaine.' I came out of my cabin to find Jim inquiring as to my well-being. He also informed me that a rule of the Friary is that if guests fail to emerge from their rooms within twenty-four hours of their arrival, their cars will be claimed by the town of Herman. His extension of kindness and outstanding sense of humor has enabled me to move beyond my shyness and has allowed me to be really present with everyone at the prayer service this evening, which is blessing me during this time of mourning."

Jennifer Kiley stated to Jim one day that "the Hermitage is my shelter in the storm and my home away from home. Jim, it was in 1987 when I first heard your story and was struck by God's gracious mercy toward you, your gratefulness, and your total acceptance of it. So, I thought, I wasn't a lost cause. You gave me hope that I too might be forgiven. I now know that I have been and I haven't been the same since."

Another person who came to the Hermitage for spiritual direction was Pat Mulligan, who became a significant person in focusing Brother Jim's ministry. In addition to being a wife and mother, she also was a committed member of the Secular Franciscans, an order founded by Saint Francis for lay people. Men and women from all walks of life, living in the immediate and greater Herman/Butler area come together for prayer and worship, to grow in their experiences of God and to support one another in their individual and corporate ministries. Pat's primary outreach was a ministry with prisoners, specifically the Saint Dismas Prison Ministry that conducted retreats in prisons. It was at the Hermitage that she met Jim, heard his story, and knew immediately of his potential for the prison ministry. She knew that since he had left Rockview he had gone back each October to lead a week-long retreat at the special invitation of the warden. At her urging he soon became a member of the conference team.

Though still integral to the daily life of Herman and to the steady stream of visitors at the Hermitage, Jim was away more and more frequently in his expanding prison ministry. Among the Pennsylvania prisons he visited, in addition to his yearly trips to Rockview, were the State Correctional Institutions for men at Graterford, the Women's Penitentiary in Cranberry, the Federal Penitentiary at Bradford, the Southwest Secure Treatment Unit (SSTU) for juvenile offenders at Torrance, the Youth Development Center in New Castle, the Mercer State Correctional Institution and the State Regional Correctional Institution (Dallas) in Wilkes-Barre, Laurel Highlands Prison in Somerset, Cambridge Springs Prison for Women in Cambridge Springs, the Federal Correctional Institution in McKean, and the Allegheny County Jail and Western Penitentiary in Pittsburgh. He also visited the Green Penitentiary in Morgantown, West Virginia.

The "Metanoia" Retreats or Missions began Thursday evening and ran through Sunday. The inmates were divided into small groups that stayed together throughout the retreat. They were seated at separate tables during the discussion periods and a member of the team was seated at each table. There were thirteen talks given during the total conference, most of which were followed by small group discussions. Personal devotions took place through the Rosary and the Stations of the Cross. Mass took place two or three times, and priests were available for confessions.

One of the talks Jim gave had to do with one's relationship with God and the reality of it in daily living. Time for questions followed the talks and Jim, along with the other team leaders, were available for individual conversations with the inmates. Each leader said these were the "richest" times.

Sitting at the back of the conference room at the Southwest Secure Treatment Unit in Torrance were Jim and Pat Mulligan and the conference team. They, along with a room full of teenage offenders, were listening spellbound to inmate Michael Vance speaking about his drug-filled years, his troubled life, and his time in the State Regional Correctional Institution (Dallas) in Wilkes-Barre. There he spent five years of his time in solitary confinement as punishment for a fight with another inmate that resulted in the inmate's death. He also spoke of his time years earlier in Dallas when the Metanoia Retreat was held. He stated that he was so impressed with the conference that he promised God that he was going to do whatever possible to bring Metanoia to his new "home" in Western Penitentiary when he got there. He had requested a transfer to the Pittsburgh facility to be closer to his mother who was in poor health. No more was ever heard of Michael's "promise."

As he continued to speak of the Metanoia at Dallas, he was so shaken that he could hardly finish. To the assembly he stated, "I still cannot get over the fact that all these people traveled such great distances to share their lives with the inmates as they are doing with all of us now. I cried for four days—the entire time of the retreat, but it was that guy in the brown Franciscan habit back there who really got to me. There was a time when Brother Jim wore the same brown prison uniform that we all wear right now. After hearing Jim I figured, if he could make it, I could do it too!" At the conclusion of the conference, as the team was leaving and exchanging hugs with Michael, he announced, "I will see you at the Youth Development Center in New Castle when you come to do the conference there. I am allowed to be on the team."

It was several years after the conference at SSTU that the Holy Name Society received an invitation to send the team to Western Penitentiary to do the Metanoia retreat. It was discovered that Michael, after he was transferred to Western, had sent a letter to the bishop of Pittsburgh, requesting that he do something to get Metanoia into Western Penitentiary. That letter was published in the prison newspaper. Mike had kept his promise and Jim was on the team, returning, for the first time, to his old "alma mater."

The Holy Name Society also met monthly in the Mercer State Correctional Institution, and at one of their regular meetings was an inmate named Robin Gates, who had a PhD in education. One day, in a fit of rage, he had beat up his young son. He was tried, convicted, and imprisoned at Mercer. One of his rehabilitation requirements was to attend anger management therapy.

While waiting for the monthly Holy Name Society meeting to begin, a short, jolly, brown-robed monk came in and sat next to Robin. In the course of the meeting, the two introduced themselves. Jim at that time, however, did not reveal his prison past and Robin did not know about it until he attended a Metanoia Retreat in the fall. There on the team was Brother Jim Townsend, out of whose mouth poured the most overwhelming experience Robin had ever heard. In retelling Jim's story to others, Robin stated, "The Holy Spirit slicked me into a relationship with himself, but also into becoming active in the prison ministry and returning to the practice of my faith."

When Robin shares his own story and tells of Jim's impact upon his life, he also includes, "I was moved at Mercer to develop a Brother Jim Townsend Award." It is an award given annually to an inmate who is an active Holy Name Society member and in good standing with the church. His Holy Name Society peers select the recipient, and it is the highest award presented to a Catholic inmate. The statement of purpose of this award reads:

Brother Jim Townsend Award

Brother Jim Townsend has been an outside volunteer for the Mercer Holy Name Society and a Franciscan brother for the past twenty-five years. His ministry covers both schools and prisons. For those of you who knew Brother Jim, he spent over twenty-two years in Pennsylvania's prison system and juvenile detention facilities. The remainder of his life has, and continues to be, devoted to our Lord. The purpose of the Brother Jim Townsend Award is to recognize an active member of the Mercer Holy Name Society who exemplifies the Holy Name Society principle and the Catholic faith.

When the news of this award reached Jim, his mind immediately flashed back several years to Rockview when he was leading his annual first-week-in-October retreat. The annual banquet, which came the last night of the retreat, was when the Casey Martin Award was given, which Jim himself had won so many years ago while still in Rockview as an inmate. The Holy Name Society had since renamed the award the Monsignor Walsh Award, to honor all that Father Walsh had done throughout the years, touching the lives of countless inmates. But during the retreat Jim was remembering, the night before the banquet, Monsignor Walsh had taken him aside to prepare him for some news: that from now on the award would be known as the Jim Townsend Award. Monsignor Walsh further said that on the following evening Jim would make the first presentation of the newly named award to its first recipient.

Jim couldn't speak. He felt that his breathing had stopped and that he needed air. He took several deep breaths to regain stability in his body while fighting the tears that wanted to take over and leave him totally out of control. *Oh Lord,* he thought. *The only way I could be who I have become is because of what you've done in me. This award says I'm supposed to be certain things and these things are what they see in me. Even those who locked me up and guarded me to protect others are honorin' me. I can't believe all this is happenin'.*

The next evening at the banquet, while Monsignor Walsh was announcing the new name for the award and talking about Jim before introducing him to make the presentation, Jim's mind and feelings were suddenly sidetracked. He was intently responding to some questions that intruded themselves. *How did I ever get to such a time like this when people are praisin' me? How could this be possible?* Then there surged through his mind, like a fast-forwarded video, the beatings from his father, being alone and frightened at eight years of age in a reform school, riding the "freights" across the country, living in hobo camps, no one really caring where he was. He remembered the anger and fights with his brother Bob, being sent away, Bob's setting him up falsely to be arrested and imprisoned, the sex orgies, the endless rage and anger, the attempted rape, Alice, the murder, the hurt he caused so many people, the nightmares, the daily violence at Western. *Oh Jesus!*

"...and now it gives me great joy," Monsignor Walsh continued, "to ask our brother Jim Townsend to come forward and make the presentation of the highest award anyone can receive here in Rockview, and...."

Jim left his seat heading for the platform. A standing ovation spontaneously filled the banquet hall and carried him to the microphone. As he began to speak, there was complete silence as every inmate listened, not wanting to miss one word. Before them stood a man who had walked their walk, who had experienced much of what they had experienced, in many instances worse, who had persevered through it all. Though still badgered by hurts and weaknesses, here was a man who was empowered to rise above them to live a life that meant something. He was their living example of hope.

Jim made his way back to his seat, briefly clasping the hands extended to him as he passed by. He sat down as the tears cascaded off the sides of his chin. *All I know, Lord, is that as of tonight, I really no longer am the man I was when I came into this place as a prisoner years ago. It is a miracle. But I also know that my feelins will never ever be able to understand your love and why you wanted to do all this for me.*

EPILOGUE

Healing and New Freedom

This account of God's working through Jim to impact the lives of countless people continues. He has been living the hermit's life now for twelve years. The last two years of this period he spent in Wheeling, West Virginia, from which he continued his ministry with the Secular Franciscans and with prisons. In 1999, before Jim moved to Wheeling, however, his health began to deteriorate. He had surgery earlier that year and then discovered that he needed additional surgery. During these months Father Lester, his guardian, became aware that Jim was afraid of dying, Jim who had been fearless all his life. Father Lester began to help him face this fear, discover its source, and thus experience the Lord's peace and presence in it.

It eventually became clear that Jim's fear of dying was connected to something unfinished in him concerning Alice's murder. In addition, there continued to nag at him an ongoing doubt that he really was fully loved and accepted by the Lord in spite of his genuine knowledge that God had forgiven him and did indeed love him. After many discussions with Father Lester, it became clear that Jim was unable to experience the fullness of God's love because he had not fully faced the truth of Alice's murder. Father Lester understood that unless a person comes to grips with the truth about oneself, he will not be able to know God's forgiveness in its fullest. When Jim would talk about his doubt about being fully loved, he would often state, "I don't want to spend a long time in purgatory after I die."

Father Lester was quick to point out that Jim knew Christ as Lord and Savior and had been living a penitential

189

life: faithful and prayerful; serving people in prisons, schools, and the community; sharing his pain and witnessing to Christ—all for the salvation of souls. Why would he question hope in his resurrection?

There were some areas of truth that Jim had to face regarding Alice's murder. The first area of truth pertained to which story of the murder was the true one and why he referred only to his own version. In newspaper accounts of the murder, a conflict arose regarding the story Jim told to the police about how the murder took place. On November 15, 1947, the *Uniontown Morning Herald* stated, "Following two months of frightening his bride of half a year, in an attempt to regain the affection he believed he had lost after she became an expectant mother, James Townsend shot and killed her at 9:30 Thursday night."

On November 17, 1947, the same paper quoted Jim as stating, "I intended to shoot just past her head or nip her in the shoulder. I was so nervous I could hardly hold a gun. I did not intend to kill her as I loved her." But Jim's account of the story that he originally told to the police and newspapers centered on his getting into a fight in a bar in Uniontown during a poker game. During the fight, three men threw Jim out the window. Enraged, he went back to the farm to get his gun, planning to return to the bar and blow them all away. But Alice, realizing what he was going to do, struggled with Jim for the rifle. It went off and she fell to the floor. Jim then went on to tell the police that he went around the property making it appear that there had been a prowler. This version of the murder is the one he has told through the years at conferences and retreats. But this story is counter to the newspaper accounts, the coroner's and the police investigative reports, and the conclusion of the court.

Why then has Jim, through the years, continued to tell this version of what happened?

It is a well-known fact that when we have a very traumatic experience in our lives, our minds and emotions go to work to protect us from things we absolutely are unable to handle. We either keep from dealing with the trauma by holding it at arm's length or by pushing it down. Or we block it out—repress it or completely bury it to the extent that it affects us unconsciously—and only therapy can reach it. There is one other thing we do and that is to put together a picture within the truth that we can live with, given what has happened or what we have done. It is an attempt to make ourselves, if possible, more acceptable to our world and ourselves. The intent is not to be dishonest, but to survive.

The story Jim has told through the years has been his way of being able to live with the overwhelming trauma he created. A key example is that he was given copies of these newspaper and police accounts in 1997, but only in late 1998 did he finally read them. Focusing on the partial truths of his version of the story enabled him to hide from the fact that the murder was not accidental. He had to face the truth of what really happened. The things he did on the farm property to frighten Alice and to indicate that there had been a prowler were done before the murder, not after, to substantiate his story.

Jim never dealt with his first twenty years of a life of violence. What he had looked for all his life was a person like Alice who loved him as he was and wanted to be with him and he with her. In his naiveté and ignorance as to why Alice was pulling away, he only knew that he could not let her leave him as every other significant person in his life had done before her. She would not be allowed to pull away from him any further. He stopped her.

An additional truth that Jim had to deal with was the account that Alice was carrying twins. At his arraignment in 1948, he had to have heard this report as a part of the trial. However, he never remembered hearing or reading about this fact. His dreams and nightmares in prison centered on Alice appearing before him with a young child. When he told his story publicly, this is what he talked about. But when at a conference in Cleveland, a spiritually gifted woman whom he had never met before spoke to him about receiving a message from the Lord indicating that he would have had a son, his story changed. But a year ago, when he was shown actual copies of newspapers from 1948, he was shocked and devastated to learn about the twins. Now in his public presentations he says, with great lament, "I have realized that I did not kill two people but three."

Having to deal with these truths has been very painful for Jim. To be able to face these things in his life required the safety of a community that practiced unconditional love and support. This he found in the Capuchin Hermitage.

Now, God doesn't bring us to some point of truth or allow us to live in the pain of a reality we've created only to leave us and let us flounder. His purpose for all of us is to set us free and to heal the brokenness and pain within. I was honored quite unexpectedly to be part of the healing that followed Jim's awareness and acceptance of the truth of what he had done.

In October of 1998 at a WorldWide Communion Sunday service at my Presbyterian church, an extraordinary thing happened. During the long, wonderful period of silence and prayer as the elements were being passed, Jim's name suddenly intruded itself into my mind. It was a moment of great joy for me as I began to recount our relationship and to thank the Lord for giving Jim and his gifts to all of us. A great sense of love poured out of my heart for him, and I felt that Jim was right there with me. At one point I opened my eyes and looked up at the communion table. I saw an opaque image of Jim from the waist to the top of his head above the communion table with the cross on the table in the center of his chest. I wasn't startled. It all seemed very natural. His image remained there until the whole congregation had received the elements. During this time I had the distinct sense that God was pouring out his love upon Jim, drenching him with it while I sat there. I saw waves of an aura of this love in slow motion cascading from the top of his head. While all this was going on, Jim was looking out at the congregation, smiling that wonderful smile. The experience of the presence of that love was overwhelming and brought tears to my eyes. But with it came an inner urgency to talk to Jim as soon as possible. When I arrived home, I phoned immediately and got the answering machine at the Hermitage. I related the incident and the fact that I had literally witnessed God's overwhelming love being poured all over him.

Jim never returned my call that day, and it was a week before I finally talked with him. I learned that he had not been emotionally able to have a conversation with me after he had heard the phone message. He could only sit in awe of the fullness of the reality he had longed to know in recent years—the fullness of God's forgiveness and love for him. He finally knew that he knew, both in his head and in his heart.